LITTLE ONE,
MAID OF
ISRAEL

by

BILL HARVEY

SCHOOL OF TOMORROW®

Lewisville, Texas

©1976 E. B. Harvey
Reprinted but not edited by
ACCELERATED CHRISTIAN EDUCATION®, INC., 1995
with permission of E. B. Harvey

ISBN 1-56265-007-6

2 3 4 5 Printing/Year 97 96 95

Printed in the United States of America

DEDICATION

I wish to dedicate this book
to the sweetest of all maids to me,
my wife,
Billie Jean.

PREFACE

Nearly 3,000 years ago in the tiny nation of Israel, situated in Samaria, there lived the prophet Elisha.

Syria was to the north of Samaria and was becoming very powerful because she was located between Persia, east of her and the Mediterranean Sea to the west; too, she was between Turkey, to the north, and Israel, to the south. All caravan travel was forced to take routes through Syria, and she received taxes from them all, giving protection in return.

In II Kings 5 is a charming story of a little unnamed Israelite maid who simply told what she knew and made a man and his family happy. In the Bible story we are told that her testimony shook two nations who might have gone to war over the matter had not the prophet of God intervened.

The little maid is not named in the Bible and I have chosen to call her Little One in my story. However, all who are known of God are named by Him. Some day we may find the quality of our witness may determine the beauty of our names.

Any name I might have chosen for this valiant daughter would most surely have proven inadequate.

If there are lessons in this book, let it teach different things to different readers; the story is the thing. I hope you enjoy reading it as much as I did writing it.

The Author

LITTLE ONE, MAID OF ISRAEL

PART I

he was barely twelve years old and small for her age, but she didn't let her size keep her from doing chores around the house that were really supposed to be done by older people. She knew the chores were to be done and there was no one else handy to do them, so she made a mental list and checked them off one at a time.

Any time other chores were caught up there was always water to be brought from the well for cooking, washing dishes, bathing, and washing clothes. Sometimes she felt like complaining about all she had to do, but she had found that complaining made the job harder and got nothing accomplished at all. Her mother often said, "The quickest way to get rid of a hard job is to do it."

She had made the beds and helped with breakfast. She had done the dishes, carried the water outside to pour on the ground well away from the house and brought the dishpan back into the house to rinse it out and wipe it dry. Then she went after more water.

Her mother was not home at the time. She had gone to the nearest neighbor, five miles away, to ask if they had heard from any of the men who had been called up by the king of Israel to serve in the army for awhile because of the Syrian raiders who would come down to Israel and carry off defenseless people and take them back to Syria, and they would never be heard from again.

If her mother had been there, she would have said, "Make sure the big water pots are filled, Little One." The little girl never let the big water pots get empty and her mother knew she never did, but her mother just had a habit of saying that and the little girl didn't mind. She never took it as fussing or nagging; in fact, it was pleasant to hear her mother's voice. It was almost a song: "Make sure the big water pots are filled, Little One."

There were six big stone water pots that stood between the front door and the big table that served for preparing meals as well as eating them. They were never moved. Little One could not have moved one even when it was empty, for it was so heavy. She could have nearly hid in one when it was empty. Of course, she never got in one because the water pots had to stay nice and clean; one never knew when the water dipped from them would be used for drinking or cooking.

Little One had a much smaller clay pot in which she carried water. She would go out to the well, a good 200 yards from the house, let the well-vessel down into the water by a rope, bring it back up and pour the water out of it into her own clay water pot and set it on her head, steadying it with one hand, and walk with it that way all the way back to the house. Sometimes it would take ten or fifteen trips to the well and back to make sure the big water pots were full.

Except for her mother's father, Reuben, she was all alone on the little farm. He was too old to go to war and his many years of hard work were taking their toll physically and he could not do much else but sit around the house. He was a good, kind old man. Like her mother, he called her Little One and seemed to enjoy talking to her when her chores were caught up. Little One loved to listen to him talk, too. He told her so many interesting things.

Little One liked to hear Grandfather Reuben talk about Moses and Joshua and how Jehovah delivered the Israelites from bondage in Egypt and brought them through the Red Sea and drowned the Egyptian army that was chasing them. His eyes would twinkle with excitement as he told story after story. Then he would quote some of the laws that God had given to Moses and his face seemed to glow with a reverence for the words he was reciting and his eyes would fill with tears. "Do you love God, Little One?" he would ask, and Little One would pat him on the shoulder and say, "Oh yes, Grandfather Reuben, I do love God."

The big water pots were finally all filled again and Little One was able to join her grandfather at the nearby table for a few minutes rest.

Old Reuben smiled as his granddaughter sat across the table from him, but he smiled only in recognition of her company. His thoughts seemed to trouble him and for a little while he sat in silence.

"Let us pray, Little One," he said, breaking the stillness, "that your mother will soon be back home, safe and sound. There are Syrian bands about in the land and our neighbors are over five miles away. Let us pray God will keep her safe." Reuben began the prayer with a voice trembling but full of faith and Little One bowed her head and silently prayed as her grandfather continued.

Little One loved to hear Reuben pray. It was when he prayed that he seemed young and strong again and she just knew God was there to hear and answer. Before long the prayer was ended.

"Grandfather Reuben," Little One asked, "why

do the Syrians come and fight the people of
Israel?"

The old man gave her question some thought, as
she knew he would, and then looked at his
granddaughter. "Our two countries have been
enemies a long time and God uses our enemies to
get us to turn back to Him when we stray. In fact,
God uses anything He needs to get His people to
turn back to Him. He is good not to give us up."

"Do you hate the Syrians, Grandfather?" Little
One asked.

"No, Little One. It is not right to hate anyone.
The Syrians are not apt to do what is right if they
do not know what is right, and they do not have
anyone to teach them. But our enemies will never
have a chance to do right if we do wrong just
because they do wrong. And it is wrong to hate."

"Why do they do wrong?" asked Little One.

"Because," answered her grandfather, "their
hearts are wrong. They prove their hearts are
wrong because they worship idols. There is only
one God. Remember what Moses said, 'Hear, O
Israel: The Lord our God is one Lord: And thou
shalt love the Lord thy God with all thine heart
and with all thy soul, and with all thy might'."
How many times Little One had heard her grandfather say those words.

"Oh, Grandfather," Little One exclaimed, "I just

don't think I could live where people don't believe in the true God!"

"Yes, my Little One," Reuben assured her, "you could if you had to. I hope you never have to, but you could. There are some that could not, but I just know you could because you know the true God in your heart and you would do what is right. The true God is in all places whether the people believe in Him or not. If you had to live in Syria, you could pray to the true God there as well as you do here."

Little One got up from the table feeling rested from the water-carrying and went over to the window on the far side of the big room away from the table and looked out.

"Grandfather Reuben!" she called, looking back toward the table where he sat, "There are riders coming on horses!"

euben was startled by Little One's announcement.

"Horses, you say? Are you sure my child?" Reuben picked up his cane and walked as quickly as he could to where Little One stood looking out at the window. Sure enough, he could see riders coming. There were eight, maybe nine. He could not be certain because of the dust they were raising.

"They are coming here!" Little One cried.

"Yes, they are," Reuben said quietly so as to calm her, "but they may be our own men. Let us wait and see. The Lord will take care of us, Little One. Now, don't be afraid no matter who they are. Be calm and polite. Good manners are always in order."

Soon the riders were there in the small yard. There were ten of them and their horses whinnied

and breathed heavily, making a bubbly sound with
their lips. Nine of the men looked to one rider who
was better clothed than they. They turned their
horses this way and that, looking the little farm
over, perhaps looking for a watering trough where
their horses might drink.

"Yes, they are Syrians," Reuben said quietly to
his granddaughter. "I will greet them at the right
time." Little One admired her grandfather's great
calm.

The lesser members of the Syrian band wore
coarse gray robes. Each man wore a sash different
from the others in color and material and it was
worn tightly about the middle. In each sash was a
scabbard that held a knife. Across the right
shoulder was a wide leather strap, thin enough to
be comfortable, but thick enough to hold a much
larger scabbard at the left side of the warrior so
his right hand could easily draw from it the great
curved blade it housed. Each rider had two
skin-bag canteens of water attached to his saddle.

The leader was different from the others only in
his clothes. He had the same dark features and the
same set of weapons as the others. His boots were
made of fine rugged leather. The others wore
coarsely woven shoes with rough leather only on
the sole. The leader's robe was a bright yellow,
tightly woven and cunningly embroidered. His

sash was multicolored and the leather scabbards were wrought with silver and set with jewels.

The front door opened, startling the horsemen. They reached for their weapons.

"Greetings, friends! And welcome to my humble farm. Won't you get down and let my granddaughter get your horses some water? Surely you are thirsty too. Come into my table and let me pour you some water."

Stark silence greeted Reuben's welcome. The horsemen looked at him, then to their leader as to what reaction they should have. The leader looked intently at Reuben. Finally, turning to his comrades he said, "Behold a cool head! He comes out to greet us as though we were Israelites." At this he laughed and the others joined in, not quite sure of the point of his joke. He dismounted and so did the others; he walked toward the door and they followed.

"Old man," he spoke grimly, "we are Syrians. Can you not see we are Syrians? Are you not afraid of us?"

"Perhaps," admitted Reuben, "but I am more afraid of not having good manners. I certainly mean no harm to you and I pray God you mean none to us."

"And what god is that, old man?" the soldier asked harshly.

"We in Israel believe there is only one true God. It is He to Whom I pray," Reuben spoke evenly and pleasantly.

"But what is his name?" asked the leader. "The name of our god is Rimmon. We have temples built to his honor in Syria. Are you saying Rimmon is not a true god?"

The leader's voice was loud and threatening, but Reuben answered softly and firmly, "Our God's name is Jehovah. It is He Who created all things."

"All right, old man. Enough of this talk about prayer and gods! We are thirsty and hungry. Do you have any food?"

"We have some bread and I think there might be some cheese." Reuben started over to the table. The leader looked around the room and then turned to the men. "Wait out here. I'll see what kind of food they have here."

Little One had just returned from the other room in the small house. "Granddaughter, these men are in need of food and their horses need water. I will see what food there is for them and you go fill the watering trough at the well."

"Yes, sir," Little One answered quietly, trying to keep the fear out of her voice. She went over to where her clay pot sat, picked it up and started to the door.

"Wait a minute, young lady," and the leader

stepped to the door. "Jamal," he called to one of the group standing nearby, "this is the old man's granddaughter. Take the horses to the well and draw water for them. We'll save you some food."

The young man took hold of the reins of a couple of horses and started toward the well; the other horses followed. Little One walked several paces ahead of Jamal, pondering the day's happenings with mixed feelings. "The Syrians have not harmed us so far," she thought, "maybe all will go well."

When they arrived at the well, Jamal dropped the reins of the two lead horses and pulled up a big vessel full of water, much fuller than Little One would ever attempt to pull up, then he poured it into the trough.

"Won't the horses run away?" Little One asked.

"No," Jamal smiled, "they smell the water and they're thirsty. They will stay."

3

s Little One walked out of the door she had taken a quick look at all the horsemen. Most of them had beards. Jamal did not.

For the first time Little One had an opportunity to study one of the Syrians closely. She guessed Jamal was the youngest of the riders. He might be eighteen, surely not over twenty. His clothes were warlike, but his face was not. Without the knives he could pass for an Israelite.

Little One placed her small pot on the stone apron of the well so Jamal could fill it, then she would carry the water to the trough and pour it in. "The horses will drink the water faster than you can pour it in the trough." Jamal laughed. His teeth were bright against his dark tan face.

Another, much larger clay pot stood near the trough and Jamal put that on the well apron. It held three times what Little One's pot held. He drew and poured four or five times and stopped only when he saw the horses wouldn't drink all he had poured; then he rested some.

Jamal sat on the well apron so that his feet cleared the ground. In a few minutes the water in the trough was almost gone and Jamal had to draw and pour three more large pots of water for the horses.

"Will the horses want to run away when they have enough water?" Little One asked.

"No," grinned Jamal, "then they will be too full of water to run much."

Jamal drew one more vessel of water and filled Little One's pot with it, then he raised it to his lips and drank deeply. Afterwards he leaned over, tipping the pot so the water would run over the back of his head; with his free hand he scratched his head, occasionally moving it so the water would hit the right spot.

"That's good cool water!" he said, wiping his face with the sleeve of his robe and smoothing his hair back with his hands. Wet with water, his hair was a jet black. "What do they call you?" he asked.

"Little One," she replied.

"Very accurate," he teased.

"Yes, I'm very small. I heard the man with my

grandfather call you Jamal."

Jamal studied her. "Yes," he said.

"Jamal," Little One asked, "have you been a soldier very long?"

"Not long," Jamal answered, "but we haven't been home in three months."

"Why do the Syrians want to hurt us?" she asked.

"Because the king says we must. It is not that we want to hurt you, but the king says we must come to Israel and get people to serve us. We are soldiers and must do what the king says."

Little One wondered how Jamal could be so dispassionate about it. "How could you do some of the terrible things you do unless you hate the people you do those things to?" she asked.

Jamal had to think that one over. "A soldier must do what he is ordered to do. I don't think I hate the people I hurt, but I have to believe I hate them when I am ordered to fight them."

"My grandfather says the Syrians do wrong because they don't know what is really right," Little One offered.

"It is right to obey the king and his officers. That's all I need to know about what is right," Jamal countered.

"But what if the king is wicked and cruel?" Little One asked.

"Then the country is in for a bad time of it,"
Jamal said as he walked over to a couple of horses,
taking their reins. "We'd better head back to the
house." Jamal started in the direction of the house
and all the horses followed the two he led.

When they arrived at the house Little One could
see the men crouched or seated on the ground in
the yard eating what she knew to be portions of
the loaves her mother had baked just yesterday in
the nearby earthen oven. Some had a portion of
cheese with the bread and others gnawed on some
dried meat her mother had been saving for a
special day. "There will not be very much left after
these Syrians eat their fill," she thought.

The men nodded to Jamal as he brought the
horses up and looped the reins of each one over a
low branch of a small tree at the corner of the
yard. After he made sure they were all secure, he
walked to the door of the house and knocked.

The door opened and the leader stood there, but
something was wrong. The leader looked over
Jamal's shoulder. "Where is the girl?" he asked.

"Looking at the horses, I think," Jamal said.

"Go bring her here and then you can eat," the
leader commanded. With a nod, Jamal went to
where the horses were tethered.

"Your grandfather wants you," Jamal told her.
He thought she would come more quickly if he told

her that than if he told her the leader wanted her.

"All right," she said, and followed Jamal back to the house.

Little One could tell something was amiss when she walked through the door. She had only barely seen the leader of the group when she left to help water the horses and her grandfather was standing near him as she left; but now, where was he?

"Where is my grandfather?" she asked the leader, trying to hide the fear in her voice. "In the room, girl," the leader said, "in bed. The old man is sick."

Little One went into the room where Reuben lay on his bed. He looked bad, very weak. She went over and looked down at her grandfather. His eyes were closed and he had not heard Little One come into the room. She stood looking at him for a full minute before he sensed she was there and opened his eyes.

"Little One," he said weakly.

"Grandfather! What has happened? You were all right when I went to water the horses." Little One knelt by Reuben's bed and put her head on his shoulder and couldn't hold back the tears. "Oh! Grandfather Reuben! What is the matter?"

The leader and Jamal stood at the door to the room. "Let's leave them alone," the leader said. As they walked toward the table he went on, "You'd better eat, Jamal. We'll be going very soon. Some Israelite soldiers may have already heard about what happened at the other farm."

"Why is the old man so suddenly sick?" Jamal asked.

"It is because of what I told him concerning the accident at the other farm," the leader explained.

"Yes," Jamal said, "Chahm was trying to ride down their watchdog and the woman thought a child was in danger. She ran to get him and Chahm couldn't avoid knocking her down."

"Yes," said the leader. "Too bad! We thought for awhile she only had the breath knocked out of her, but her head had hit a stone. She was dead. I told the old man about it. It was his daughter! He had me describe her, what she was wearing, you know. He said he was afraid it was his Leah and then clutched his chest as though he had a great pain. I called some men in and we carried him to his bed. I haven't told him, but that's the name the other women at the farm kept wailing over the woman, 'Leah! Leah'!"

Back in the room Reuben was speaking softly to Little One. "Don't cry, Little One. I am soon to be gathered to my loved ones in Paradise. I am not suffering any more, my little granddaughter."

Little One sobbed, "What will I tell Mother when she comes home? Oh, do not die, Grandfather Reuben!"

"You must listen carefully, my sweet one. There has been an accident at the farm your mother visited today. The Syrian leader told me of it. Your mother is not coming home. She was killed, Little One. I did not want you to hear it from the lips of an unbeliever. She is with God. She did not suffer." Without any bitterness Reuben told her all about the accident, patting her little head gently with his work-gnarled hand. He let her cry for a time on his shoulder, but then he felt he must say some other things to her.

"Darling Little One, now in all this time of sadness you must remember clearly all you have been taught. Remember that God will take care of you. He is everywhere and He will take care of you. Pray to Him every day and ask Him to make you a blessing wherever you are. Look at me and promise me that, my Little One!"

Reuben's words were like a birthright to Little One. It was as though she was one of the sons of Jacob whom he blessed. The solemnity of it and the richness of his words called her out of her heartbreak, for she must make a promise.

Her voice was steady now, almost grown-up. "All right, Grandfather Reuben. I promise I will always remember all I have been taught and I will pray daily to the one true God,"

The old man smiled. "Good! Good! That's it.

Now say with me once more the blessed words of Moses."

Little One knew well the passage Reuben meant. They recited in unison a portion from the Fifth Book of Moses' writings: "Hear, O Israel: the Lord our God is one Lord: And thou shalt love the Lord thy God with all thine heart, and with all thy soul and with all thy might."

Little One had looked away during the quoting of the Scripture, and when she looked back on the face of her aged grandfather she could see his spirit had left his body.

With a new maturity Little One went into the next room and stood at the door until the two Syrians saw her standing there.

"I believe my grandfather is dead," she said simply.

ome here, child," the leader said softly. Little One walked to the table where he and Jamal were sitting. "I am sorry. Stay here with Jamal while I go see for certain your grandfather is dead." Jamal and Little One watched the leader as he went to the other room.

The leader was back to the table in just a moment. "Yes. He is dead. Are there other men in the family, child?"

"Yes," answered Little One, "my brother. He is away, serving for awhile in the king's army. My father died of fever a year ago."

"Where is your father buried?" the leader asked.

"Beyond the big tree to the north. The grave is marked," she answered.

With that the leader stepped to the door and motioned to two of the men who were looking toward the door, and they came. The leader spoke quietly to the men for a few moments. One of them went to three of the others and they came into the house. The other man untied one of the horses and rode toward the big tree- some 300 yards in the opposite direction from the well.

The four men who came into the house went to the room to wrap the remains of Reuben in the sheet he was lying on and reported back to the leader when they were finished and went back into the yard. Shortly the rider who went to the grave site also returned.

"I found the place," he said to the leader.

"Good," the leader answered. "Get some men and tools and dig a grave for the old man. We want to leave by nightfall."

Little One had been standing silently since she answered the questions about the burial place of her father. Jamal studied her. The sun's rays came into the west window at the far end of the big room from the table and seemed to fasten on the form of the little girl.

He thought, "The face has a certain resoluteness and calm not seen in many children. Most her age would have been completely distraught, so grief-stricken we could have gotten absolutely no information out of her, but she stands calmly in the midst of all this as though she were prepared. It's unnatural."

Jamal's thoughts were interrupted by the voice of the leader speaking to Little One.

"Little One," she answered.

"Well, sit down, Little One." Little One sat down on her end of the bench at the table across from Jamal and not over five feet from the leader who was standing.

"Did your grandfather tell you about the accident at the farm near here?" the leader asked.

"Yes," she said, her tearless eyes seeming all the more sad, "he told me."

The leader hurried to explain: "No one wanted to hurt her! One of our men was chasing a dog and a child almost walked into the path of his horse. Your mother ran and pushed the child from in front of the horse and was knocked down. We didn't think she was badly hurt at first, but she had struck her head on a rock. I'm sorry. She was very brave."

Now the tears were flowing down the cheeks of Little One and she brushed them away with her sleeve. The two men waited while she regained her composure.

"It is God's will. I understand," she finally said.

"Soon the grave will be dug," thought the leader, "and we can bury the old man and leave this place. I do not like this business of attacking defenseless farms and kidnapping women and children. Company against company, army against army—that's what I like."

He paced back and forth between the table and the room where the dead lay and continued his thoughts: "What kind of child is this that she can hear of the death of her mother and see her grandfather die within an hour, and yet behave so bravely? What is to be done with her? She has no family. Who knows what has already happened to her brother? He may already be dead. We cannot leave her here. We cannot take her back to the other farm. We must take her with us."

Little One got a small bowl from a shelf near the big stone water pots and dipped it into the nearest pot and drank from it. Afterwards she dipped it again and wet a small cloth in the water, squeezed the cloth and wiped her eyes with it. "I must wash the vessels," she said.

"Yes, Little One," said the leader, "that would be good." Then to Jamal, "Go gather the bowls and cups the men have used and bring them in." He thought it would be better for Little One to be doing something; it might dull her sorrow. He watched her as she poured water into the large pans and thoroughly washed the cups and pots and dried them, then put them where they belonged. After that, she took the damp cloth with which she had been washing the vessels and wiped the table.

Before long, one of the men came to the door and told the leader the grave was finished.

"All right," said the leader, "there is a short ladder at the fig tree. Get it and we will use it to carry the body to the grave."

"You need not go, Little One," the leader said to her, "my men can see to the matter."

"Oh yes," said Little One, "I must go to the grave with him. I am his only loved one to be there."

Next to the door of the room where Reuben lay was a large box with a lid on it. Little One walked over to the box and opened it and took out a large black, sheer veil, loosely woven with fine wool. "My mother wore this when father died with the fever." Little One wrapped it around her head and under her chin, bringing one end of the veil across her face so that only her eyes could be seen; then she went to the bench at the table and sat down again to wait.

Some of the men had padded the ladder with blankets and quilts and put the sheet-covered form of Reuben on it and carried him out of the house.

"We shall proceed in this fashion:" the leader explained. "The girl and I will walk in front; you four men will follow with the body and the rest of you will lead all the horses after us." He was taking no chances an Israelite patrol would surprise them at the grave.

The small procession arrived at the site of the open grave and the four men bearing the body set about to remove it from the stretcher and lower it into the grave. "Gently!" the leader commanded softly. Soon it was done and the men stepped back awaiting further orders. The others were in the shade of the tree with the horses.

"These men will fill the grave with dirt now. Let us go back to the house." The leader turned to go toward the house, but Little One didn't move.

"I must pray," she said.

It was not a request. The leader simply nodded agreement and stood still. His men also kept quiet.

"Dear Lord," Little One began, "thank You for letting dear Grandfather Reuben live so long. He has trusted You for many years and has taught us all to trust You; and now he is gathered to his loved ones, as are my mother and father, but because of my trust in You, I do have hope of seeing them again. Now give me strength to live as they taught me to live. Amen."

Little One turned and walked back toward the house and the leader walked beside her. The four men who had carried the body to the grave began filling the grave with the mound of dirt that had come out of it. Their horses were left there for them, tied to a low branch of the huge tree. The rest of the men followed Little One and the leader on foot, leading their horses single file. The simple burial had had its effect on all of them.

hen the procession arrived back at the house Little One went in and the leader turned to speak to the men. "Find provender for the horses. We will be leaving when the others have finished with the grave and have seen to their own mounts. It is better that we travel at night. The Israelite patrols have been active the past few days." Turning to Jamal he said, "Feed my animal. I must speak to the girl."

The leader waited for several minutes before going into the house, thinking Little One might want to freshen herself or be alone for some reason. Finally he knocked.

Little One came to the door and opened it for him. "May I come in?" the leader asked. Little One nodded, stepping back, opening the door wider. The leader came in and sat on a stool near the table. "Sit down, young lady," he said, motioning toward the table bench. The bench was higher than the stool and when she sat down their eyes were on the same level. "You are a brave girl, Little One," he said. "I have never heard anyone pray as you prayed awhile ago at the grave. You really do believe in this God, don't you?"

"Yes, I do," said Little One.

The leader looked into her eyes and could find there only sincerity. "We will be leaving very shortly to go back to Syria. You must come with us, Little One," he said.

Little One had been wondering what she would do. She had eaten the morsel or two of bread that had been left by Jamal and saw that there was nothing more left to eat. While she was alone in the house she had prayed that God would direct her steps and show her what she should do. She did not really want to go with the men, but she must do whatever the leader said.

"Couldn't you take me to the farm my mother went to this morning? Must you take me all the way to Syria? My brother will not know what has happened to me." Little One showed no fear. The leader admired this in her.

"No," he answered, "taking you to that farm is out of the question. They may have already contacted an Israelite patrol. You would starve here by yourself. We must take you with us. As for your brother, I shall leave him a note. Can he read?" The leader looked around for something on which to write.

"Yes," said Little One, "my brother can read."

The leader spied a large flat unfinished clay tray and set it on the table. "Perfect!" he said as he took his dagger from its jeweled scabbard. He scratched a bit on the corner of the tray to see how much pressure he would need to make the letters. Then he wrote: "The woman Leah and her father are both dead. We have taken the girl with us and she will be well treated." Then he read the words to Little One while she looked at the tray. When he read the words, "she will be well treated," a look of confidence came to her eyes. The leader saw it and was glad. She would be much easier to care for if she went willingly.

"There you are," he assured Little One. "Whoever comes into the house will surely come to this table and they will see this message. Now you get some things you wish to take with you and we will soon be leaving."

Little One understood that she could not take very much, so she would have to be careful to take only her best and warmest clothes. It would be cold as they traveled at night, so she simply put a heavier robe on over the one she was wearing. That way, she wouldn't have to carry it. She took two blankets, laid them on the bed stretched out, then laid two dresses on the blankets along with a favorite sash and shawl. Then she rolled the blankets up with the other things inside them and tied them with some leather thongs very securely.

When she was certain she had everything ready for the trip she put the blanket roll on the table and went around closing and locking the wooden doors to the windows. After she could think of nothing else to do she sat down by the table and waited.

The leader had gone out to make sure his men had fed the horses; soon he came back in. "Ah, you are ready, I see." He was glad there would be no delay. "Perhaps you should include a cup and a bowl with your things. We will be at least four days getting home."

"Yes, I will be needing those things," she said, and fussed silently with herself for not having thought to get them. She hated to undo the blanket roll. Wait a moment! Reuben had a large leather pouch with a strap on it. She could put the things in that.

6

he sun was already down and twilight was mixing with moonlight as the Syrian patrol cantered steadily across sandy fields, grassy slopes and rocky paths, heading for the small mountains situated to the north and east of the farm house. Little One had never experienced the cold night air rushing at her face as she rode in front of the leader, but it did not keep her from wondering if she would ever see the little farm house again.

"I'm glad that God is everywhere," she thought. "Though Syria should be a hundred days away, He would still be there. Grandfather Reuben had not shown any bitterness when he was telling me about Mother Leah getting killed; he had such a deep conviction that God's will is more important than anything else. What had he said to me when Father died and then my brother was called to serve the king? 'The surprises of life cannot hurt as much if you remember God is never surprised.' I asked him what that meant so he put it another way: 'Often we do not know why things must happen as they do, but we are comforted when we know our God knows why because He knows all things.' It is so very strange how close Reuben seems when I can remember his words and the sound of his voice. Yes, his voice went with his words; they were both peaceful. That was the picture of dear Reuben. In Syria, when I want to remember Reuben I shall think of 'peace'."

"When Father died," Little One remembered, "neighbors came from five different farms to comfort the rest of us and I overheard some say they were astonished that Grandfather and Mother were not helpless with grief, but instead, Grandfather was singing Psalms of hope and Mother was smiling. I will miss Mother, too, but I shall miss Grandfather more. Until the last few weeks he would walk with me to the well and back and teach me a Psalm or tell me how he felt about some part of life in his own special way. He had such a way with words; you could easily remember what he said because his words were put together just right."

Thus did Little One while away the riding hours of the night. They would ride two hours and rest a half hour, usually by a stream or pond. The leader would go with the men and leave Little One to refresh herself with water from the brook; he saw that she had complete privacy.

The Syrians and Little One reached the grassy approaches to the mountains just as an outline of light could be seen over the hillocks. This particular route was not very familiar to any of them and they could not make as good time as when on the worn paths. Soon the horses were walking.

As it grew lighter one of the riders with a keener eye cantered up to the leader's horse. He pointed to the east. "Sheep," he said. The band stopped. In a few minutes everyone could see them. Without good light they could be mistaken for boulders on the hillside. There were at least 200 in that one flock. "You know what to do. The girl and I will stay here. I doubt the shepherd would miss just one out of so many." The men nodded and rode carefully toward the flock of sheep so as not to startle them. The sheep stirred but none ran. Soon two sheep dogs sent up a warning so the men rode toward them. It was growing much lighter very quickly and they caught glimpses of the dogs running first toward them and then back to a little lean-to shelter below where the sheep were gathered.

The shepherd called the dogs back to him and

quieted them with a little scolding. Now the Syrians could see him just beyond the lean-to.

"Ho! Shepherd!" a Syrian called.

"Hello there!" the shepherd called back. "Can I be of any service to you, sirs?"

"Indeed you can," assured the one called Chahm. "We are a hungry band of soldiers and we are in need of one of your lambs for breakfast. Will you choose one for us?"

"Sirs, I cannot," said the shepherd. "They are like children to me. How can I choose one for death?"

Chahm turned to the others. "There, my friends, you have the noble shepherd. He cannot decide which animal to let us have." And then to the shepherd, "Is it not better, shepherd, to give one of the lambs to die so that the lives of all the others be spared?"

"Yes, I'm sure that is better, but it is hard for me to choose the one that must die." The shepherd saw his predicament. He did not want to die. These men had weapons and were on horses. They could kill many sheep just by riding through the flock and he could not stop them, but he would die before he chose the lamb that would be their meal.

Chahm was a fierce, bearded veteran of many battles. He was as short on patience as he was gentleness.

"Shepherd!" he bellowed. "Will you die needlessly? If you do not choose a lamb, we will kill you and take what we want!" He was the oldest in the Syrian band and considered himself the hardest of heart. As he reached to take the sword out of the large scabbard at his left side, he saw a slight motion just behind him and to his left, and a good-sized lamb lay dead four paces from him with a knife in its throat. It had not made a sound.

"There!" hissed Jamal, "I have chosen the lamb!" He lit swiftly off his horse, grabbed up the lamb, taking the knife from its throat, and threw it over the front of one of the rider's saddles. The dogs started to dart for Jamal but a little kissing sound from the shepherd's lips kept them close to him.

"Let's go cook some breakfast," said Jamal, as he remounted and started back to where the leader and Little One were waiting.

With a slow gallop the nine horsemen soon reached the leader and Little One. "We must dress and skin the lamb soon;" said the leader, "there is a likely place up ahead to make camp."

None of the men spoke to the leader about how the lamb was obtained; he didn't care to know. But Chahm let the other riders get ahead of him until he was back with Jamal.

"Hey, boy!" Chahm said grimly. "You do not

like the way I dealt with the shepherd?" His jaw muscles were flexing.

"I didn't want you to kill the shepherd." said Jamal. "There was no need of it. What would have happened to all those sheep?"

"Just the same, boy," murmured Chahm, "don't ever do that to me again!"

7

 place was chosen for the camp farther up into the foothills; a place high enough that all approaches to it could be seen by one guard on watch and where a good fire could be kindled for cooking the lamb. Jamal and the rider who carried the lamb went off a good 300 yards from the campsite to dress and skin the animal, leaving the entrails and fleece for the carrion. By the time they arrived back at camp there was a nice fire going with a frame fashioned of hard, dry wood on which to turn the lamb to roast above the flames.

It would take an hour for any part of the lamb to be cooked enough to eat and someone must turn it so that it would not burn.

"Zogaht," said the leader, turning to one of the younger men, "you tend the fire and the lamb," and to another, "Jahl, you keep watch on that high boulder, and see you stay alert!"

The small, skin, water canteens each horse carried had been filled at the last stream they had forded before daylight. Each man tethered his horse ten paces from camp and then gathered plenty of wood for the fire. Then they carried their saddles to a spot that suited them, not too far from the fire. There they arranged saddle and pallet for sleeping and, before long, the fire-tender and watchman were the only ones awake.

The leader had watched as Little One spread her blankets, taking the space left over after everyone else was settled and was curious as she stood a few moments with head bowed facing away from the fire. Soon she lay down and wrapped the blankets tightly around her and was asleep.

Little One was a light sleeper, even though she was very tired from the night-long ride. It could have been the movement of one of the horses or the unusual gust of cool air to her face, but she awoke suddenly. The fire was nearly out and the young man Zogaht was sitting up, but his head hung down in sleep. Little One slipped quietly out of her blankets, went over to the pile of brush and wood and chose some pieces suitable for getting the fire going again from the red embers; she placed them with the small bits of brush against the embers and the larger pieces over those, then she got down on her knees and blew the coals softly until the brush was crackling and flaming again.

When she was sure the fire was going well again, Little One wrapped herself again in her blankets and faced the fire to see if Zogaht would stir.

Zogaht stirred with a start as one will when he knows he should not be sleeping. He knew he had been asleep, but he did not know for how long. The lamb on the spit was bubbling and needed turning. Realizing he had nearly allowed the fire to go out, depriving the patrol of food made him wide awake again. He grabbed for the turning stick and was pleased to see the lamb was not burned any place.

As he slowly turned the lamb, stopping at intervals to put large pieces of wood in the right places on the fire, he pondered his narrow escape. If the leader had caught him asleep, there would have been some punishment for sure and he would not have been too popular with the other men either.

"Just how long was I asleep?" he wondered. "Someone rebuilt the fire for me, but who? I hope the leader will not think I have taken too long to cook this lamb. Perhaps he will notice it is unusually large and take that into account. But who replenished the fire?" Zogaht eliminated each comrade, from the sleeping leader to the man on watch. "No, the leader would shake me awake and ridicule me before all the rest. The others, any of them, would be happy to see me get extra duty. It would just relieve them of some distasteful task. I must ponder it some more; but one thing for sure, I will not fall asleep again."

No one had stirred since Little One rescued their breakfast without their knowledge. Now the lamb was a juicy masterpiece. The day was getting warmer and the lamb needed no further cooking. Soon the leader stirred and threw his blanket from around him. Sitting up, he called to Zogaht, "How's the meat?"

"Just right, Leader," Zogaht answered. They had slept two hours.

The camp was immediately a beehive of action, each man doing things necessary to such a life. The smell of the roasting lamb soon brought them with knives ready to slice off a portion.

"Jamal slew the animal," said leader, "let him have first cut." All agreed. Jamal crouched down and cut two portions and handed Little One one of them.

"Thank you," she said.

"Jamal," said the leader, "when you are through eating, go and take Jahl's place on the rock. He'll need some food and sleep." Then he assigned others their watch time until mid-afternoon when all would have had enough sleep.

Mid-afternoon came and three of the men were sent to scout the area at hand to see if there were food for the horses and water for everyone. A half hour saw one of the three bring word that both were near. It was a natural pool on the side of the mountain that caught the melting snow and rain that ran from rocky crevasses. Through the years, soil also had washed down from the upper reaches and plush green grass grew from it. The same water that filled the pool fed the grass.

Each man took the saddle and bridle off his horse. The horses were hungry and could be counted on to stay where the grass was plentiful. The horses seen to, each man filled his canteen with water and drank his fill, making sure the canteen was filled when he was through with it.

Little One stood away from the others, waiting until she might get near the water. She had her cup in her hands.

Zogaht happened to be the first to notice her standing there waiting. All of them were used to seeing only to their own needs. He walked over to her. "Let me have your cup and I'll fill it for you." Little One silently handed him the cup.

As he was kneeling down at the side of the pond to get water from the cleanest area it suddenly dawned on him who had saved their breakfast and most likely his neck. The little Israelitish maid!

He walked slowly back over to her, not wanting to spill the water, and handed her the cup.

"Thank you," she said.

"No," smiled Zogaht, "thank **you**!"

And Little One just smiled at the ground.

LITTLE ONE, MAID OF ISRAEL

PART II

1

n Damascus, Benhadad the Mighty was looking out over the city from his favorite window in the Great Hall of the palace. Yesterday and the day before the **khamsin** had blown in from the desert, making life miserable; you dare not open a window during the **khamsin**, but now the hot wind had subsided and the sun shone upon all the dust-laden roofs beneath his gaze. Mentally the king implored his god Rimmon for rain to wash the city again.

Benhadad enjoyed being king and took his office seriously. He was respectfully rotund. Who would want a skinny king? His face was round and pleasant, and wore a thin mustache and small goatee. He enjoyed the finest of clothes from the bazaars and wore large rings on most of his fingers...rings presented to him by caravan masters who wished to impress him. He had a wife somewhere about the castle, but he was more interested in affairs of state than in being a husband, and they were not often seen together. He was in his early forties and had the gift of being excited about everything he did.

Benhadad reviewed his latest accomplishments with satisfaction. He had every important caravan owner brought before him and, with the aid of his chamberlain, had exacted good tribute from them, promising them protection from bandits along all routes from the valley of the Euphrates and Tigris Rivers and the Persian Gulf in the east to the Nile River and the Mediterranean Sea in the west. With such diplomacy he had more than satisfied his major merchants by stipulating that each caravan would display its wares for those merchants before proceeding east or west. What a happy arrangement! Damascus abounded in factories and founderies, producing brocade and swords. Some of the copper brought from Persia by a caravan going west would be elegant cups and bowls, ready to be sold back to that same caravan coming back through Damascus on its way to Persia. How commerce satisfied the subjects!

Yet, in all his exultations there came a shadow to his countenance. The Israelites! They have no diplomacy or even politics, for that matter. There is no dealing with them. A treaty is nothing to them and there is no conquering them. With them it is no army against army; they are obliged to get the word of some holy man in siege or challenge.

"Chamberlain!" he called back through the hall. The Great Hall echoed the word down the passage-way to the diplomat's chambers. He hastened to the Great Hall.

"My lord, the king!" he said to Benhadad, calling him away from the window.

"Did you send word to all the Syrian patrols to return home?" the king asked.

"Yes, sire, except those escorting caravans through Samaria to the sea. Some are arriving every day; most are empty-handed, but some bring booty and captives," said the chamberlain.

"Good!" observed the king. "And tell me, is Naaman any better?"

"O king, I am grieved to say the Captain of the hosts is not any better but still remains in isolation from the soldiers and his family. He is able to ride within a stone's throw of his house so that he might see his wife and children from a distance, but he dare not get closer. He gives verbal orders to those under him. Sometimes he resorts to drawing military tactics on the ground with a stick and retiring fifteen or twenty paces where he can call the explanations of them. The man is a genius in such matters and is popular with his men. Much of the booty brought back by the patrols goes to his wife at their home on the Abana."

"That is good. I myself have directed that such treasure go to the dear lady. She has suffered greatly, being deprived the company of so great a man. Oh, that devilish leprosy! Is there a greater plague?"

"No, my lord, I think not," replied the chamberlain.

"What is being done for this man?" asked the king.

"Your majesty," assured the chamberlain, "Jaichim, the physician, is his constant companion; every caravan master coming through Damascus is questioned thoroughly about a possible cure. Many ointments are tried, many potions mixed and prescribed, but to no avail. We offer rewards to every traveler if he will bring something from afar he has heard to be effective. We keep trying."

I would sell this palace and give its price to the physician or herbist who could deliver Naaman of his disease. He would otherwise be a perfect man," the king declared.

Walking over to the window again to look out upon the narrow streets and mottled roofs he turned once more to the chamberlain. "You may go," he said. The chamberlain bowed with a murmur of respect and left the Great Hall.

Back at the window the king stood with hands behind his back looking at everything and nothing in particular. His thoughts were fastened on Naaman, the general of all his armies. "Oh," he thought, "there is much a king can do, but so much more he cannot; I cannot in all the kingdom find wherewith to comfort Mahrrah and her children. Only a well husband and father can comfort them."

hen it was discovered that Naaman had leprosy, the king ordered that a house be built at one of the lovely sites along the Abana River. The melting snows from the Anti-Lebanon Mountains fed the Abana through a narrow gorge in cataract proportions in spring and early summer, but Naaman's handsome house was situated safely at the top of a grassy slope with a full view of the mountains, the rushing water of the gorge and the river. One need only walk a bit to the right and a hundred feet above the gorge to see Damascus.

No luxury was spared and every suggestion by the builders that promised more comfort to the dwellers was adhered to. Great cedars were brought up from Lebanon for main supports and struts. Ingenius troughs and gutters were devised to bring water from a sparkling spring to placid cisterns where liquids and produce could stay cool. The cistern had a spout that could be lowered to let its cool water run over into a pot or bowl.

There were more than enough rooms in the great house for each of its four occupants to have two apiece. Each room was furnished lavishly, but in good taste. A cottage nearby housed the servants.

The favorite room for all was the huge living room with its stone floor and animal skin rugs and elegant carpets. A great fireplace took the middle third of the north wall of the big room and servants kept the fire going day and night in winter with huge logs. The architects planned doors and windows for good ventilation. A porch where the children could play in bad weather was fashioned from half way on the south wall to the northeast corner of the house.

* * * * * * * *

Kurd, the patrol leader, had already purposed in his mind that he would see if Naaman's wife would like Little One to be one of her servants. It would not be as though she was being treated like any ordinary captive, for indeed, she was not. The leader had not ceased to be amazed at the little girl from his very first encounter with her. He would not be just selling her to a slave merchant, as was his right, with the king's permission, of course, but he would be giving her to the wife of the most famous man in all Syria, excepting Benhadad himself, and he would feel better knowing the child was in lovely quarters. She would most surely compliment any household.

Little One had been no particular trouble to him or the patrol. In fact, when she had learned the routine of camping and caring for the horses she was as much assistance as any member of the band. The journey back to Syria with her was uneventful and he was pleased to hear all patrols were being called in except for the caravan escorts.

After reporting to Command he took Little One to his home. He had told Jamal to come to his house in two days and that he would have something for him to do.

"Well, who have we here!" Resha, his wife exclaimed.

"One of those big bad Israelites, my dear," said Kurd, "whom I have conquered with great cunning and fortitude!"

He plucked Little One from off her perch quite easily and even she smiled at the leader's little joke.

"Kurd! The little child must be worn out," chided Resha, forgetting all else for the moment.

"If she is," said Kurd, "I doubt that either of us

would ever hear her say so. I want to keep her here for a couple of days so we can get her rested and bathed and perhaps find some decent clothes for her at the bazaar. I have in mind taking her to Naaman's wife, Mahrrah."

"But Kurd, where did you get her?" Resha asked.

Little One had not heard his name before. The others had only called him "Leader" to his face or "the leader" to each other.

"Where and how I got this little Israelite makes quite a story, but you shall not hear one exciting part of it until you put some food before the two of us." He winked at Little One. "You see, young lady, a soldier must be forever foraging for food, even in his own home." Little One knew what it was to forage for food.

As they ate, true to his word, Kurd told the story in detail. Resha could see that Little One had made Kurd a different man. He had left for Samaria a coarse, hard soldier and had returned as pleasant as an ambassador. She mused to herself, "My husband seems more the captive than the captor, but whatever she has made of him, I like it and I can't help but love this little Israelite."

Kurd recounted the accidental death of Leah and Reuben's death and funeral and Resha could not keep the tears away. "Oh, you poor, poor child," she whispered, but Little One patted her hand and said, "It is God's will, dear lady." Resha hastened away from the table to look out the window. "God's will," she murmured, dabbing her eyes. "Will you listen to that?"

Kurd told it all. He even told about Little One saving their lamb after their first night's ride. Zogaht had finally told it on himself when trying to outdo the others in praising Little One when they were nearing Damascus. He related how she would gather all their canteens and fill them with water while they were asleep or occupied with their horses or she would rub down the saddle and bridle of a horse while its rider was on watch. "She was never in the way," Kurd bragged, "and she never complained. How I wish I could say that about my own patrol!"

Resha said to her husband, "You are right. She will make a good servant for Naaman's wife."

The rest of the day and evening were devoted to woman-talk between Resha and Little One with a trip to the bath house and trying on clothes. "Ah, me!" Resha said. "You are so tiny. I don't have a thing in this house that will come near fitting you, but wear this garment for now and I will wash your best gown and you can wear it to the bazaar where we can find something for you."

Little One liked Resha and complied with every wish.

"I declare, Little One," exclaimed Resha, "you are the most pleasant little creature I've ever known. Don't you ever get angry?"

"Yes," replied Little One, "but mostly at myself."

Resha put Little One to bed and started out of the room; then she heard something behind her that made her turn around. Little One had thrown back the covers, gotten out of bed and was kneeling beside it.

"Is there anything wrong?" Resha asked.

"No," answered Little One, "I was just going to pray."

"Little One," said Resha softly, walking back toward her, "would you mind if I stayed while you pray?"

"I wouldn't mind at all," she answered.

"Dear Lord," she began, "thank You for keeping us all safe on the journey from my home and for letting me be with kind people like the leader and his wife and for a good bed to sleep in tonight and for the good food we had today. Bless these friends through me. Protect my brother, wherever he might be and protect us all as we sleep. Amen."

As Little One opened her eyes she saw Resha sitting on the foot of her bed with tears on her checks.

"Oh, Little One," she said, gripping her hands in

one of hers, "if there is really a one true God Who is everywhere, He surely must have heard your prayer tonight."

"Dear Resha," said Little One, her dark brown eyes opening wide in assurance, "there really is a one true God and I know He heard my prayer."

Getting up from the bed, Resha patted Little One's forehead and brushed her hair with her hand. "Good night again, little maid of Israel. Tomorrow is a big day."

3

ittle One did not know how tired she really was. The kindness of these people who were supposed to be her enemies had surely kept her from knowing how tired she was. She slept the whole night through in her own bed. When she awoke it took a moment for her to realize where she was. Odors of things cooking told her Resha had already been up for some time and the sun had been up a good while too.

Little One popped out of bed and washed her face in a basin on a table near the bed and dried on a towel, then, after making sure her hair was presentable she went in to say, "Good morning!" to Resha.

Resha had heard Little One stirring and already had her food on the table. "Go ahead and eat, Little One," she said, "I've washed your best gown and I'm trying to get it dry near the fire. Kurd has been up a long time and is getting a cart for us to go to the bazaar when we are ready."

The food was good. She didn't know what kind of meat it was but thought it better not to ask. It beat anything they had on the trail. The figs were especially good and she had never eaten bread quite like that either. When she had finished, she told Resha how much she had enjoyed it and declined more when Resha offered it.

Soon all things were ready for them to leave the house. The gown was dry and smoothed, the vessels were washed and dried and everything was put in its place.

"Are you women ready?" Kurd called, stomping into the room, more to make his presence known than to dust off his boots.

"We are ready and have been waiting," Resha winked at Little One, but Kurd caught it and retaliated, "and suppose I told you I could not get the cart and we must all walk to the bazaar?"

"I would then call you a liar," Resha countered, "because I saw you out the window driving it past the house."

"Then I shall not tell you that. Let us be going!" Kurd said.

It was a new world to Little One. She had never smelled such odors, seen such costumes, ridden such streets or heard such sounds. Merchants and customers haggling excitedly, wood and steel on cobblestone, vendors pleading for people to come in, all attacked her ears at once, but she was delighted.

Many of the merchants recognized Kurd and Resha as friends of Naaman and called to them to stop at their stand, but Kurd knew exactly where he wanted to go and did not slacken his animal's pace.

In about the same time it took Little One to eat breakfast, the cart made the trip to the bazaar. Servants were there to see to everything. One assisted Resha and Little One down from the cart; another helped Kurd down; still another took the horse and cart to the nearby animal stalls, but all knew Kurd. His military bearing brought instant clapping of hands and slave's obedience.

Passing by the hired sellers, Kurd went over to where three owners were passing pleasantries. They saw him coming.

"Kurd!" they all chorused, "We are honored by your presence!" The one called Tawfik smiled and said, "Are you coming to buy from us or do you bring something for us to buy?"

"That is right," said Butros his partner, "you never know whether Kurd is coming to buy or sell after one of his trips." And they all laughed.

Wadi, the quieter of the three offered, "I know Resha, your wife, but who is this little girl? I have never seen her before, that I can remember."

Kurd thought to have a bit of fun at their expense.

"She is from Samaria; an Israelite maiden whom I took captive during my last campaign," he explained.

The three merchants stopped their smiling and looked intently at Kurd, trying to find whether or not he was joking. If he were not joking, here indeed was an opportunity for profit, for the market for slaves was never satisfied.

Resha punched Little One lightly with her elbow and Little One followed the conversation with great interest.

"We are here to outfit my little captive from head to toe." Kurd informed the merchants. "I have decided to bypass the trader and go directly to a very wealthy prospective buyer myself. I figure she will bring a much better price if she is dressed well. Don't you agree?"

"You are a cruel man of war," chided the quiet one, Wadi. "You prepare the damsel with our own clothing and cheat us out of added profit by selling her yourself. What would your command say of your new sideline?"

Kurd was enjoying the piqued tone of his

favorite merchants.

"Oh, indeed," offered Tawfik, "and it would be criminal of us not to warn you of the pitfalls of such a venture. Slave trading is a very specialized field. I might as well try soldiering!"

"Ah, yes," added Butros, encouraged by that line of thinking, "and there is no more tragic sight than a merchant trying to be a soldier than perhaps a soldier trying to be a merchant."

"But brothers," pled Kurd, the soldier, "are you not my friends? Could I not come to you for advice in this business venture and obtain your assistance? Are you not my friends?"

"Of course, we are your friends, dear Kurd," cooed Tawfik, then turning to his partners, "Have we ever seen our soldier brother depart for a campaign without burning incense to Rimmon?"

"Never!" declared Wadi, "and the last time you left I paid a merchant ten stalls down to make an offering to his god Ashur. Why take chances?"

"And right now," said Butros, spreading his hands and holding his head to one side, "right now we are proving what friends we are by begging you not to enter into such a demanding business without the proper qualifications!"

"Enough!" cried Kurd. "Am I going to have to go elsewhere to clothe my little captive?"

"But nay," soothed Wadi to Kurd and to his

partners, "he is our friend; let us see that he has at least the proper attire for his merchandise."

All three merchants led the way to the garments and began making suggestions simultaneously. Resha rescued Little One from their pawing and measuring and picked up this gown and that, this robe and that.

"Your wife," said Tawfik softly, "knows her merchandise quite well, but isn't she a bit extravagant in her choice of things?"

"I don't believe so," Kurd replied. "Money spent on clothes will be more than doubled in the price of the slave."

"Ah-ee!" complained Butros, "he's been listening under our tables and has not gone to war at all."

"How's that?" Kurd asked.

"Nothing!" said Butros. "Nothing at all."

Soon Little One's wardrobe was complete with two of everything and it came time to tally up. Resha had taken her to a chamber adjacent to the stall and put one complete change of garments on her. Then she brought her back into the store.

The merchants greeted her with great admiration. "She is a wonder! Kurd, what were you expecting to get for her? Perhaps you still need a middleman. Name me a price, hey?"

Kurd ignored him.

"Do you know what those clothes are going to cost you? You will do well to break even. A slave never wears clothes like that!" Wadi began figuring with gestures and grimaces. "That comes to exactly three gold pieces and four shekels copper."

"Now," laughed Kurd, "I see why you prayed for my safe return: so you could break me financially! I cannot see more than two pieces of gold in the entire wardrobe."

"Then you are blind, my soldier friend. Someone poked you in the eye!" cried Wadi.

Haggle and bargain! Offer and counter-offer! Finally the price was settled.

"Thank you so very much, gentlemen. You have made this young lady look as presentable as she ought to." Kurd started for the street.

"What do you mean, 'thank you very much'? You have not paid the agreed price!" cried Wadi.

"Think with me, brethren. How much have you made from goods and captives my patrols have brought you from afar?" Kurd hastened on. "I did not go to another stall. I did not allow my soldiers to go to another stall and you have taken us, man and boy, for more shekels than we could make up in a life time."

"A bargain is a bargain and business is business. We cannot cry over last year, can we?"

Tawfik reasoned.

"All right, merchants," smiled Kurd, "I have had my fun." The partners all chuckled in relief. "I am not going to sell that girl."

Tawfik chortled, "Did I not tell you, brethren, the fellow could be a politician as well as a soldier?"

"Yes," laughed Butros, "and much better than a slave trader!"

Even Wadi entered into the merriment unrestrained. "Benhadad needs you in his court, not in his army!"

"Now perhaps you will sell the girl to us that we might make an honest profit?" suggested Wadi, growing suddenly solemn and drawing the others close to him.

"Gentlemen, allow me to assure you that if I were going to sell this little lady, I would sell her to no one but you, my esteemed friends." The merchants glowed. "But as I told you," Kurd continued, "I am not selling her." Then he might as well have overturned their tables when he said, "I'm going to give her to someone."

A moment of utter silence. A time of looking at one another in total disbelief. All were unable to find a word among them.

"Ah-ee! Bu-, bu-, bu-! Y--y--y--!" But Kurd did not let them get set before he attacked another flank. "And that is why you are going to **give** those clothes to the little lady. I am giving this little Israelite to the wife of Naaman, Captain of the King's hosts!"

The merchants walked away in three different directions, all talking to themselves, imploring Rimmon, cursing the first day they ever made a transaction with this thief.

Finally, they all converged back to Resha, Little One and Kurd. Kurd knew what they were thinking. If he had told them at the outset he was giving the girl to Naaman's wife and wanted clothes for her, the merchants would have given one set of much cheaper garments, but Kurd had masterfully gotten their minds on his reckless venture into slave trading and they allowed the finest to be put on Little One. Now if they tried to take the merchandise back, word would get out they had mistreated a gift to the most popular figure in all Syria, save the king. It would ruin their business! They would have to leave their families and go back to caravaning.

The three came close together, all looking sourly at Kurd, postponing the inevitable agreement, none daring to voice it.

"Let me make you feel better, comrades of the bazaar," Kurd smiled.

"How can you?" said Wadi, not changing

expression; he saw nothing to smile about.

"I will say the gift is from the four of us: Kurd the soldier, and Wadi, Butros, and Tawfik, the most famous merchants in the bazaar." Kurd waited for his proposal to take its effect.

Wadi pulled on his beard thoughtfully. Tawfik looked back and forth at Wadi and Butros. Butros had a silly smile on his face. But it was Wadi who finally put their feelings into words. "Brilliant!" he bellowed. "Who could ask for better advertising?"

Tawfik saw it too, but couldn't do anything but laugh until he cried.

Butros still wore the silly smile, but nothing got by him. "This man has out-tricked us and we are laughing about it!" he said.

"Yes!" cried Wadi, "But, he has made us partners in the most generous of gestures. You must agree we would not have a gift of ours looking shoddy."

Tawfik could only roar and point at his partners, one at a time and at Kurd. Resha and Little One grinned broadly at the whole thing.

Coming over to Little One, Wadi looked down at her and said with a touch to her shoulder, "Little maid of Israel, you are a gift from us to the greatest soldier in Syria. The better you work for him and for his family, the better our gift will be. Will you work well, or will you be a lazy gift?"

Wadi expected no answer, so he was surprised to hear Little One say to him, "I will work hard and try to be the best gift possible, sir, and thank you for the beautiful clothes."

This destroyed Butros. "Did you ever hear a slave talk like that one?" he hollered.

"No," said Wadi, "nor a gift!"

The soldier, his wife and the maid left in the cart to go back home. The three merchants stood at the entrance to the bazaar and watched their progress, glad to see them go.

"I know we are poorer," said Wadi, "but I somehow feel richer." And the others agreed.

In the cart rode the soldier as though returning from a fresh campaign. Beside him sat his wife looking at him and smiling. Next to her sat the little maid of Israel looking radiant in clothes utterly foreign to her.

"Say!" said the soldier's wife, "I did not know I was married to so shrewd a businessman! Stay home from the wars, businessman, and become a patrician. Then we could afford our own maid of Israel!" And they all three laughed.

4

ebel ed Ben was the highest river site east of the gorge. It meant "Mountain of Ben." It had been a gift from the king. Referring to the high hill as a mountain and saying it was of Benhadad was a compliment tokening their estimation of the gift. Anyone within a mile of the gorge could not help but see the great house on the crest of the nearly round hill. A few sheep were kept around to cut the abounding grass and serve as pets for the children.

Djena was six. The sheep were not as frightened of her as they were of the other children. Something in her voice assured them she meant only to feed them or watch them. Khalil was eight and very boistrous. The sheep had only to sense his presence and they would run away. They could never be sure what he had in mind. Sabra was only three. He was never around the sheep unless his mother held him. He was as frightened of them as they were of him.

Sabra had never seen his father up close. He had never been held by his father. Djena could faintly remember Naaman swinging her around and holding her close at times. The memory freshened when he would ride within hailing distance on his fine Arabian and she could see his great black beard and fine white teeth as he smiled.

Djena noticed her mother was always very sad for several days after such a visit.

"So very near," Mahrrah would say, "and yet, so far!" but not to anyone in particular.

Sabra would ask, "Why cry, Mama? Why?"

She would hold him all the tighter and sigh, "You would not understand, my pet."

Khalil had his own pony, another gift from Benhadad. He was riding around the house, up and down the hill, making sure not to scare the sheep. He had been scolded enough about that. On the crest of the hill he spied riders and a cart making their way up the gradual incline of the north road. He rode quickly to the back door of the great house, fancying himself a courier with important dispatches. He jumped off his steed, tied it to the hitching post and ran into the main room where his mother was playing with Sabra.

"Mother, there are people coming from town!" he reported excitedly.

"Oh?" said Mahrrah, getting up and finding a shawl, more for the wind then the cold. "Who on earth?" she puzzled.

"One looks like Jamal," answered Khalil.

"Yes, it may be Jamal," said Mahrrah. "I heard he was back from Samaria." Jamal was her second cousin, but he didn't often come to Jebel ed Ben.

"Could you make out anyone else?" she asked Khalil.

"No," answered the boy, "but would you like for me to ride down the road and come back and tell you?" He was excited at the prospect.

Mahrrah smiled at him. "You may ride down and meet them, but don't leave them if it is Jamal. Just ride back up the hill with them. It would be rude to do otherwise. However, if you get close to them and do not recognize anyone, ride back up the hill and tell me."

Kahlil was gone in a flash. Now he had a reason to ride. He would show those people how he and his pony could go down that hill!

Yes, it was Jamal all right. He would have to ride slowly back up the road with them. His pony was grateful for that.

"It's Khalil, isn't it?" asked Jamal. "I'm your cousin Jamal," he added.

"Yes, I'm Khalil," said the small rider.

"These are friends of mine," Jamal told him. Any further explanation to such a small boy would have been out of place.

Khalil took his place behind the cart where it was most polite. Besides, it gave him a better chance to look the strangers over without their noticing. "The man on the black horse is a soldier," he thought, "but I don't know him; and I wonder who the two ladies in the cart are. I hope Mother lets me stay close when they explain all this."

Quite suddenly they were at the crest of the hill. A sharp left turn saw them in the back yard of Jebel ed Ben. Mahrrah was standing on the small roofless back porch, holding Sabra. A woman servant took the child from her so she would be unencumbered as she met her guests.

"Jamal!" she called. "Get down, won't you!"

"Mahrrah!" said Jamal, bowing slightly. Kurd had dismounted and servants had assisted Resha and Little One as they got down from the cart.

"I would like very much for you to meet my commanding officer, Kurd," Jamal said. Kurd bowed graciously.

"The ladies," Jamal continued, "are Resha, my leader's wife, and Little One, a maid of Israel." The two nodded a greeting and Mahrrah invited them into the house. As they followed her into the big room they all looked upon the furnishings and materials of the room with delight. They had heard of their splendor but were not quite prepared for it. Mahrrah got them all seated and drew a small chair to the center of the half circle so she would not miss a thing.

"How lovely to have guests at Jebel ed Ben!" exclaimed Mahrrah. "Especially friends of Jamal," she added.

Kurd knew she was filled with curiosity so he was anxious to get to the reason for their visit. "Madam," he began, "your esteemed husband has no greater admirer in all Syria than your humble servant. I can be certain any favor bestowed upon you and your family would be the same as bestowing it upon him. You are no doubt acquainted with the good merchants of the bazaar: Wadi, Tawfik and Butros?" he asked.

"Yes," she answered, "I have made purchases from them."

"They and I have brought you a gift," Kurd explained. Mahrrah looked around for whatever it might be but saw nothing and hoped they hadn't noticed her looking.

"On our last campaign in Samaria," Kurd started, "circumstances caused me to come into possession of this young Israelitish maid. The more of her qualities I have seen the more I have been persuaded she would be a worthy addition to your staff of servants. As you can see, she is dressed lavishly by the merchants I mentioned so she would presentable to you.''

Mahrrah was nonplussed. She couldn't get it all put together. "Do you mean this little child?" she asked. "I already have children.''

Embarrassed silence closed in on them. Kurd had thought Little One would have been accepted graciously and no more said about it, but what now?

Resha came to the rescue. "Oh, Kurd! Must you always sound like a soldier? You men go out and look at the Abana while Little One and I talk to Mahrrah.''

"Good!'' thought Kurd. "Anything but this.'' He got up and motioned Jamal to go with him.

"You go with the other men, Khalil,'' said his mother. The words, "other men," softened his disappointment in not getting to hear what Resha might have to say.

Resha launched right into a lovely translation of what Kurd had told her the first time she laid eyes on the little Israelite. She explained Little One's qualities and quandaries, evincing both admiration and sympathy from Mahrrah.

"Oh, you dear, homeless girl. I did not mean to

make you feel unwanted. You are indeed a lovely gift and we want you right here at Jebel ed Ben."

Mahrrah excused herself for a moment and stepped to the kitchen down the hall. "Gherza," she said to a woman servant some five years older than she, "get Abu to gather all the servants in the back yard; I have someone I want all of you to meet."

"Now you must plan to stay for supper," she said to Resha when she returned to the big room. "It would be too late for you to eat anything after getting back to Damascus."

Resha gratefully agreed and, after many more questions and answers which gave rise to more questions, Gherza told Mahrrah that Abu had all the servants together.

All of them went out to where the servants stood, all six of them, counting Gherza.

Jamal, Kurd and Khalil had found Djena around front with a lamb, holding it. She put it down gently when Khalil told her they were going to the back of the house. She didn't want to miss a thing.

Little One's cursory glance told her there were four men and two women. Mahrrah did not have to call them to order. Every eye was upon Little One, but they listened to Mahrrah.

"Servants!" she quieted them pleasantly. "This is Little One from Samaria, a captive maid brought to me as a gift from Patrol Leader Kurd and some merchants at the bazaar. I want you to welcome her to Jebel ed Ben."

"Little One," said Mahrrah, turning only her face away from the group of servants, then looking at each servant she named, "this is Gherza and that is Abu; they are married. The other girl is Mehkel. The three other men are Alexis, Rafat and Joseph."

Mahrrah was in no way prepared for what came next.

"Joseph?" said Little One softly. And again, "Joseph?" the little unbelieving question.

A tall, very thin young man stood at the corner of the small group, partially hidden from view by the one called Alexis. He seemed unable to respond. His lips were moving, his body was shaking, but he seemed unable to move his feet. His eyes were swimming with tears. Finally he burst out as though coming to the surface of the Abana.

"Little One? Is it really my Little One?"

It was an enchanting moment and no one dared break the lovely spell. They all watched silently and motionless as brother and sister embraced.

es, it was Joseph. He had been a prisoner for five months and was so distraught without word of his family he had hardly eaten. Abu oversaw the work of the men and sympathized with Joseph, but he urged him to eat as much as he possibly could.

"Joseph," Abu would say, "you must understand my position. If you do not eat, you will not have the strength to do what is required of you and our mistress will be displeased with me."

Joseph liked Abu and did not wish to cause him trouble.

Ah, but now Little One was here! Their tears of joy were mingled with tears of his newly-learned losses, but they comforted one another.

Joseph listened as Little One recalled each detail of God's providings and he took fresh faith. Her story answered many questions he had been asking the Lord and gave him a new insight to the many times his own life had been spared. Now he felt life surging up within him; now he wanted to eat everything in sight.

Mahrrah declared that evening and the next day a holiday for all the servants and was delighted to see brother and sister so animated in their happy conversations. "Oh," she thought, "if only I could embrace my Naaman as Little One embraced her dear Joseph!"

As Joseph and Little One walked and sat and soaked up the blessedness of reunion, a cloud came between them.

"Isn't God good to let us come to Syria, Joseph? I once told dear Reuben I didn't believe I could live in a place where people did not believe in the true God and Reuben said I could if God wanted me to." Little One was smiling, but Joseph was not.

"Little One," he said softly, yet vehemently, "you sound as though you are glad to be in this heathen land!"

"I am, Joseph! How much longer would I have had to wait to see you if God had not brought me to Syria?"

"But the Syrians are our enemies. I hate them!" Joseph declared.

Little One was shocked. "But Moses commands

us to love even our enemies. Reuben said we are not to hate anyone. Reuben said that if anyone could make us hate them then they would have control over us. Surely you can't mean you truly hate the Syrians, Joseph!"

"I most certainly do!" he vowed.

"How can you hate anyone as kind as Mahrrah? She is so sad without her husband," reasoned Little One.

"Little One," said Joseph, looking his sister fully in the face, "I believe it is the justice of God upon Naaman for dividing so many Israelite families. He has been ruthless and merciless against us. I hope he dies a leper!"

"Oh, Joseph," Little One choked, trying to hold back the tears, "you can't really be saying that. Tell me you don't mean it!" Little One slumped to the ground and sobbed.

"Tears on so happy an occasion?" It was Abu's voice. "What are you crying about, little maid? Is it because you are so far from home? We are all far from home, my dove," he said soothingly, "but it is something we must all learn to live with. We are slaves. We are property. We are not our own."

Joseph gripped Abu's arm. "I'll never get used to it. I refuse to get used to being another man's property! I wish them all dead!" Then he walked off toward the servant's cottage and Abu reached down and picked Little One up to stand on her feet.

"Give him time, little sister. Your brother has a great emptiness in his heart. Perhaps you can fill it." Abu and Little One walked toward the cottage and saw Joseph disappear into the men's side of the little building.

The servant's cottage was a good dwelling, as slave dwellings went. It stood at the northeast corner of the main house and ten paces away. There were three rooms in the entire cottage. A porch divided the men's dormitory-like room from the ladies' and ran all the way from the front of the cottage to the back, giving the porch a tunnel-like effect. The men lived on the east side and the women the west. Partitions had been put up in the northern portion of the women's side, making a room for Abu and Gherza with their own door off the porch.

Its simple comforts revealed the relative compassion Mahrrah had for her slaves and she encouraged them to fix up their living quarters as nicely as they could, often giving them a bit of money and permission to go to the bazaar to make a purchase when she overheard some expressed desire. She never entered the cottage unannounced but asked when would be a good time to come over.

Little One had put her things into the cottage with Mehkel. There were sleeping accommodations already and Mehkel was glad to have her company.

Mehkel was seventeen. Tall and of full figure, she was still feminine. She was from Persia. Mahrrah herself had purchased Mahkel from a slave trader soon after it was learned Naaman had leprosy.

Little One's eyes were still red from her disagreement with Joseph, and Mehkel noticed. Mehkel thought Little One might be homesick and sought to comfort her.

"Little One," she vowed, "I'd rather be a slave right here at Jebel ed Ben than any place I know. I am well-treated here. You must not cry, Little One. Be thankful you have found your brother. There are two brothers and a sister of mine somewhere in this world and I do not have a prayer of ever knowing where they are."

Little One could see Mehkel's sincere concern and it touched her. "No, I do not weep for home or even that I am a slave. I know I am most fortunate. Joseph and I are all that are left of our family, so where Joseph is, that is home for me, but it is the hate my brother has for the Syrians that I weep."

"Well," offered Mehkel, "it is only natural that a slave hate his owner. However, he should not discuss it too freely. He could be sold as quickly as a balky mule and Joseph could get a far worse master."

Little One looked at Mehkel as she sought for just the right words to say. "Joseph and I were taught we were to never hate anyone; not even our enemies. God will not bless us if we do."

This perplexed Mehkel. "You worship a god who blesses you? I have never known of such a god. The gods of Persia and those of other countries where I have been have only cursed. None of them were ever known to bless."

"We fear our God, too," explained Little One, "because He created all things. He is not made of stone or wood or metal. He is everywhere and He knows all things, even what is in our very thoughts. I can pray to Him wherever I am, even right here in this room, because He can hear me. He was the One Who brought Joseph and me safely to Syria and reunited us."

Mehkel was astonished at such words from so small a girl. "What is the name of your god, Little One?" she asked.

"His name is Jehovah," answered Little One. "His name means 'The Eternal One'."

he weeks and months went by.
Mahrrah could not believe Jebel ed
Ben was ever without Little One.
Little One kept the children occupied
with stories and games and she would teach them
songs that delighted them. The sound of singing
was unusual at Jebel ed Ben. On occasion Mahrrah
would bring all the servants in after supper and
they would sit on the floor near the big fireplace
and Little One would willingly sing the songs of
her homeland.

The songs Little One sang were not trite, foolish
little rhymes, but they were mostly of Jehovah and
His benefits. The hearts of her little audience were
softened by the sincere ring in her voice and the
radiance of her love for God glowing in her face.

"Joseph, sing with your sister!" the others
would beg, but Joseph just solemnly shook his

head and sat still.

Joseph did his work and did it well; hard work was no stranger to him, being reared on the farm. He was efficient and Abu could see he had an orderly mind. He could see the obvious thing to do and if Abu gave him several things that would occupy him for the whole morning, Joseph would set about getting the things done in the same order and manner Abu would have done them himself. Too, Joseph could read and do sums. Abu would often take him to Damascus with him to buy food for the household and stock. His quick ciphering saved time with the merchants and put them on the defensive so they knew they were in for a minimum of haggling with no chance of cheating Abu as in other times. Abu was acquainted with most all the merchants in the main bazaar and they admired him as the trusted steward of Naaman's affairs.

Now it was again time for Abu to replenish supplies for Jebel ed Ben and he asked Mahrrah for permission to take Joseph with him again. "Of course, take Joseph, Abu," she assured him. "You need not ask for permission each time." But he always did.

"And Abu," Mahrrah said, "this time the two of you take Little One with you, and take this letter to the merchants Wadi, Tawfik and Butros. It will be good for Little One to be with her brother and away from the children for awhile."

As was her custom, Mahrrah gave Abu and Joseph some coins of their own above necessary expenses. She had already given Little One some money of her own and Little One was looking forward to the trip with great excitement.

Joseph hitched a horse to the big cart and soon they were on their way.

It was Little One's first trip back into Damascus since coming out to Jebel ed Ben and it brought a rush of remembrances; her time in the home of Kurd and Resha and the strange time at the bazaar. The competing cries of the merchants, the sounds of the animals, the outraged protests of the customers all filled the air and Little One wondered if she could be around it every day as were the merchants. Jebel ed Ben was so quiet; the loudest noise was the water rushing through the gorge at the foot of the mountain.

They soon arrived and were cordially received. Abu thought it best to deliver the letter to Wadi, Tawfik and Butros first; then after all purchases were made, they could reach home.

As usual the merchants were in the back of the store, planning the demise of some unsuspecting associate or discussing their individual genius for separating a man from his money.

They saw Abu and Joseph right away but did not see Little One until they were well into their greetings, all talking at once.

"Good day to you, Abu and Joseph! You honor our humble...why, why, it is the little maid of Israel, our gift to the wife of Naaman!"

Tawfik glowed, then said in mock pain, "Look, brethren, those lovely clothes Kurd stole to put on her back! No. Don't look!" they all laughed at themselves, for the matter had become a choice trade secret among the merchants when, in an unguarded quarrel they had reminded each other of it in the presence of competitors, but they were good sports about it and Kurd had become quite famous because of it with all the merchants becoming very wary of him though still admiring him.

Abu reached into the pouch carried in the folds of his robe. "Here is a letter my mistress Mahrrah commanded me to deliver to you."

"Hmm. A letter, you say? From the wife of Naaman herself!" Wadi took the letter and the other two got close to him. "Read it aloud, Wadi. Surely we can all hear it," said Butros.

Wadi scanned the letter and a pleasant smile crossed his face. He read the letter.

"Esteemed Merchants of the Bazaar, Wadi, Tawfik and Butros: Forgive me for not having written you before now to thank you for your lovely gift of the priceless jewel from Israel. However, it is good that I have waited until now to write to you my thanks because it has given me opportunity to learn the true value of the gift. All the money in the bazaar could not buy her from me. She is the light of Jebel ed Ben. You and Patrol Leader Kurd could not have given me and my household a more excellent treasure. Thank you again. Mahrrah, Wife of Naaman."

Each of the partners took turns scanning the letter, then all at the same time began modestly taking credit for the whole idea. "Did I not say...?" "If you will but remember...." "Yes, I know, but it was I...."

Finally they thought to turn to Little One. Wadi bent down to her, putting his great grin close to her face. "I can see by the letter you lived up to all my hopes that you would be the finest of gifts to the gracious Lady Mahrrah." And his two partners nodded unanimous approval.

Abu broke in. "Masters, has it ever been told to you that Little One found that her brother had already preceeded her to Jebel ed Ben?" They were astonished. "Yes! Joseph here is her brother!" This declaration was followed with many exclamations of "Amazing!," "Fantastic!," "The gods were kind!" The merchants were obliged to greet Joseph anew as though they had never met him, glowing in the wonder of such a marvelous coincidence.

They had come to admire Joseph in the few transactions they had made with him, and now, just to think he was the brother to this flower of Samaria, their gift to Naaman!

Before long they extracted Joseph's account of how he came to be in Syria and they were delighted to see how happy Little One was to be with her brother. Oh, they would have the bazaar buzzing with their translation of this story, with embellishments of their own, of course!

"After you have completed your shopping for the day, Abu," requested Wadi, obviously the senior partner and spokesman for the others, "come back to this shop that we might give you a reply to this lovely letter."

Assurances were given and good-days said and Abu with Joseph and Little One began walking through the market. They had left their cart and would make all their purchases, then come back later with the cart and have the items put on it. At times Little One would be with Joseph and other times with Abu. Sometimes she would look at various goods in another part of the store away from whoever might be dealing with the merchant at the time. Even though she was small, her lovely clothes indicated she was a person of some means and not a waif who could not be trusted.

Joseph had crossed the narrow street to see how good their supply of grain was for bread and cakes. As was often the case, the back door to the store was the front door to the merchant's living quarters. Hanging strings of beads was all the partition present between the store and house and Joseph was looking at some samples of grain in bags near the door. The merchant was near the street with another customer and it appeared he would be tied up for awhile.

Joseph could hear voices just beyond the beads. He could not see who was talking and they could not see him. He was not deliberately trying to listen but he could not help but hear some words now and then. "Assassin," "Naaman," "Benhadad," "murder." Surely, those talking were unaware their voices had gotten so loud.

"The caravan people call the king's demands extortion. Shazzar, owner of the largest caravan coming from Persia, is paying Kursh and Djeel to come from Aleppo, and kill Benhadad. It is all settled!" one said. "Shazzar feels another king could not be worse."

"I think we should warn the king. The levies are fair. They make a little; we make a little. Who suffers?" the other observed.

Joseph was not sure there were only two of

them. The first argued, "Sure, we can tell the king and what guarantee do we have that we will not be accused along with the guilty?"

"Yes," agreed the second speaker, "it is indeed difficult to know what is right to do." Then, "Do you know how they plan to do it? What has Naaman to do with the matter?"

"The idea is to accuse Naaman of planning the whole thing. He represents total loyalty to the king. To answer your first question, Kursh and Djeel are to be hidden in the banquet hall where the chamberlain is to have a great banquet to honor the king. The deed will be accomplished that night. Just how, I do not know; in fact, I do not care to know."

The two who were talking were soon gone. They had left by another exit from the house. Joseph did not see them, nor did they see him, but their conversation had shaken him. What was he to do? He was but a slave. Who would take his word that the conversation had even taken place?

He could not say that he actually loved his enemies, but Little One's happiness and Mahrrah's love for her had softened him. He did not want the king killed or Naaman unjustly accused. The two men he had overheard seemed not to have any part in the Persian's plan and he had not heard how they came to know it. What was he to do?

Joseph started to rush quickly away but thought better of it. The merchant was coming in from the front of the stall. All Joseph could think to do was to make some marks with his fingernails on his shopping list...marks that would mean something important to him after the shopping was done: Shazzar, Kursh, Djeel, Aleppo.

Now the merchant was approaching Joseph. "And may I help you?" he asked.

7

ll transactions were completed. Necessities were tallied and set aside to be picked up with the cart and a few things were bought by each of the three servants. Little One remembered each of the children with some little trinket; Abu had bought a lovely shawl for his wife and Joseph had finally gotten the boots he had saved for since he first came to the bazaar with Abu.

All of them went back to the cart stalls situated near the store of Wadi, Tawfik and Butros. Before they got the cart however, they remembered to see the merchants again as they had requested.

"Here, Abu," Wadi said, "is the letter to the Lady Mahrrah and a small package for her also. Ask her to please read the letter as soon as possible. Take great care with the package; it is our finest brass missor." Abu thanked him.

Tawfik stepped forward ceremoniously. "And here, Abu, is the brocaded belt of fine silk just for you. We appreciate your business." Abu bowed graciously.

"And Joseph," said Butros, "we have not forgotten you. Accept this leather wallet in which to carry important documents on errands for the Lady Mahrrah. I can see she relies almost as much upon you as on Abu to transact business for her."

Joseph gratefully accepted with a glance at Abu who saw his concern. "You are correct, masters," said Abu, "and none could be more pleased than I. Joseph deserves it." He looked the wallet over. "It is a fine wallet, Joseph," he said unselfishly.

"Now what shall be the gift for the gift?" And all smiled at Wadi's play on words as he beamed at Little One. Tawfik and Butros nodded with smiles, eyes closed, hands opened before them, palms upward in jestures of mock bewilderment.

"We have looked the store over, Little One," said Wadi, "and found this!" And he whipped from behind his back a pair of earrings the likes of which Little One never knew existed. Abu and Joseph marvelled at them. These were not cheap baubles. These were earrings of finest gold encrusted with two small diamonds on each piece, sitting like bird eggs in a folded nest of silver. Abu and Joseph bent closer, mouths agape. Little One could hardly bring herself to touch them.

The merchants grinned and elbowed each other knowingly. "Do you wish to put them on your ears, my pet, or had you rather wait until you are back at Jebel ed Ben?" Butros asked.

"Oh, sirs!" exclaimed Little One, "I shall wear them if you like; that is, if you do not mind." She could detect the donors were anxious to see the rings on her ears.

Wadi held a mirror for her to remove the tiny earrings that had been placed there before she could remember and put the elegant ones in their places; first one ear, then the other.

"Ah, behold!" said Butros boisterously, "were they not meant for her?" All agreed.

Wadi kept holding the mirror for Little One to look at these precious gifts for some time. Finally she looked away from the mirror and looked at the merchants. "You are too kind to me, masters." There were tears in her eyes and the rest of the time was spent in reassuring her it was something they just wanted to do; really nothing; something they had come upon in the store. Abu knew full well they had spent a good part of the day going through a caravan newly arrived from Persia to find such earrings.

After many bowings and scrapings they were on their way. Abu asked Joseph to get the cart and

down the street they went, all three on the big seat
with Little One in the middle and the men on the
outside so they could jump down easily to pick up
their sacks and parcels waiting at the various
stalls and stores.

The gifts of the merchants, especially the dazzling earrings they gave Little One, plus making
sure every bit of merchandise was picked up had
made Joseph almost forget the conversation he had
overheard in the grain shop. In fact, it was only
when he hopped down off the cart to load up the
grain he had bought there that the conversation
came back to him. He had marked the names of
the conspirators and the town of the assassins on
the list Abu had given him. Soon the last sack was
on the cart and Abu was guaging the position of
the low-hanging sun and the amount of time it
would take them to get back to Jebel ed Ben. With
the touch of the reins on the horse's back and a
clicking sound with his tongue, Abu had the cart
going at a good pace while the road was still fairly
level; he would like to still have a bit of light left
for the long climb up the north road.

"Well, young people," said Abu, "it has been a
profitable day for all, hasn't it?" Joseph and Little
One agreed.

"That is a fine belt, Abu," Joseph observed.

"It is indeed, but the merchants were not stingy

when it came to your wallet either," Abu declared.

"That is true," agreed Joseph. Then he winked at Abu. "But it is easy to see who they thought deserved the best."

"Yes," Abu said, winking back, "it is the sad fate of being a man." All this was wasted on Little One. She just smiled. "Let them tease," she thought.

What neither of them knew was that Wadi had not read all the letter from Mahrrah to the merchants. The portion he had failed to read gave instructions for them to find earrings for Little One costing a certain amount and charge it to her account. But what Mahrrah did not know was that the merchants had matched her amount and Little One received earrings as fine as any Mahrrah ever wore.

"The bazaar was pretty busy today," said Joseph.

"Yes it was," agreed Abu. "I understand some of the chamberlain's household were there preparing for the banquet to be given in the king's honor." This sobered Joseph's countenance considerably.

"When is the banquet to be given?" Joseph asked.

"I heard someone say it was tomorrow night," said Abu. Joseph pondered the matter for some time. Abu could see he was in deep thought and the conversation had stopped so suddenly Abu felt obliged to ask, "Why, Joseph? Why would you be interested in any banquet given for the king?"

"I will tell you when we start up the north road. There are too many people who might hear what I have to say now." There were no houses on the long straight incline and Joseph could see whether or not there was anyone near enough to the cart to hear even though one talked quite loudly.

It was a half mile up the north road and the horse could go no faster than a walk. It was all right; Joseph wanted plenty of time to tell Abu everything he had heard and give him time to think of some solution to the problem before they arrived at Jebel ed Ben.

Before they were half-way up the long incline of the north road Joseph related the conversation in the grain store, carefully and accurately, patiently repeating phrases and names for Abu's many questions.

"Joseph," Abu said, "I'm glad to see your concern for the king and for Naaman. It says your bitterness has passed."

"Yes, Abu," said Joseph, "when I heard the men talking, I knew it would be an awful thing for anyone to put himself above the king. I know now that God has ordained Benhadad to be ruler of

Syria, and I believe God has used Naaman to chasten the children of Israel because of our wickedness. God has always used our enemies to call us back to Him."

"Oh, Joseph," said Little One, "I have been praying you would see that. Dear Grandfather Reuben said the very same thing to me the day he died."

Abu looked at the brother and sister. "This God of yours is something, I must say. He certainly sounds like a God worth knowing."

"He is, Abu," said Joseph, "He really is!"

heir shopping trip ended, the trio reached the house to divide sack and parcel to where they belonged; this to the feed bin, that to the house. Everything tallied. Abu gave a report to Mahrrah along with money left over and the letter from Wadi, Tawfik and Butros, expressing their desire that she read the letter as soon as possible. Little One very cautiously came in and let her earrings be seen while giving the children their gifts.

"Little One!" Mahrrah exclaimed sincerely, for she knew instantly the merchants had tricked her in a most generous manner, "Where did you get those gorgeous earrings?"

Little One flipped them lightly with her fingers and smiled. "The three merchants, Wadi, Tawfik and Butros gave them to me, ma'am," explained Little One. "You should see their gifts to Joseph and Abu," she added.

Mahrrah admired their wallet and belt. "It seems you had a wonderful day in Damascus," she said. Then after chatter and patter she noted, "Gherza has supper almost ready. There will be time for more talk later."

Little One set about getting herself and the children ready for supper while Mahrrah went to her room to read the letter from the merchants.

"Esteemed and Respected Madam:" it began. "Your benevolent thanks to your humble servants for the maid of Israel was received with great appreciation on our part and your appraisal of the young lady is noted most joyfully. She is indeed a jewel most rare and lovely. We are ever in Patrol Leader Kurd's debt for having given us an opportunity to be included as benefactors in the bestowing of such a gift to such a matrician as yourself." Mahrrah smiled at their exaggerations and read on.

"Dear Lady, some information has come into our possession; information of a most serious nature. We three merchants have received word of possible harm to the king and false accusations against your esteemed husband." Mahrrah's eyes narrowed with apprehension and she retraced the sentence to make sure she read correctly. "Harm to the king? Danger to my husband?"

The letter went on, "Your trusted servants, Joseph and Abu are aware of this intrigue and are probably very anxious to tell you about it. Because we know that Joseph or Abu always go without fail to a certain grain store owned by a cousin of one of us, we arranged for them to overhear the gist of the assassin's plan as we know it. We have learned that it was Joseph who went to the store on this trip.

"It was thought that you would have an access to the king we would not have and that the three of you could come up with a plan that would both stop such a heinous crime and bring the conspirators to justice.

"Please let us know if there is any way we can assist you in this matter. We are your humble and obedient servants, Wadi, Tawfik and Butros." And so the letter ended.

Mahrrah thought for some time upon the scroll she had just read and reread, planning what her immediate course of action would be. She saw no need to disturb the whole household. Abu and Joseph would not divulge such matters to the others, nor would Little One. Immediately after supper she must have a meeting with Abu and Joseph to discuss the best course to take. Not knowing the contents of the letter and believing she was not aware of the intrigue they surely must be anxious to speak to her in private, she thought.

Except for Little One, all the servants ate in the big kitchen. She, of course, helped in feeding Sabra. Before long, supper was completed and the necessary chores done in short order.

Abu and Joseph were in the barn, seeing to the stock. "We had better ask to talk to Mahrrah as soon as possible," Abu suggested.

Checking once more to see that everything had been done, the two finally turned up toward the house, each thinking how Mahrrah might receive this news.

They waited at the back door while Abu's wife went to tell Mahrrah that Abu and Joseph wished to speak to her. Gherza soon returned and led the men to the south porch where Mahrrah stood waiting for them. An almost full moon made the porch light enough for conversation and Mahrrah did not want to run the risk of anyone overhearing what they had to say.

After greetings Mahrrah began talking. "Joseph," she began, "did you and Abu wish to discuss with me the conversation you overheard in the grain store?"

Joseph was amazed and so was Abu. Their faces showed it as they looked at one another.

Mahrrah smiled at their expressions. "The merchants arranged that conversation at the grain dealer's, knowing one of you would be able to overhear it. As it happened, it fell your lot, Joseph, to be the one to go there. They made sure you heard everything. They felt the particulars of this matter would be better carried in your head than in a letter. Now tell me exactly what you heard the two men say."

Joseph related very accurately the plan and the names of the assassins from Aleppo.

"So far," Mahrrah explained, "we have no certain proof that the chamberlain is part of the conspiracy. He has never favored my husband, but he has never appeared to be his enemy, either. Getting word to the king is not as simple as it may appear. If I gave each or both of you a scroll to give to him, you would be searched and soon the scrolls would be the knowledge of too many people."

Abu suggested, "Could you not ask the king to come to Jebel ed Ben for some particular reason?"

"No," said Mahrrah. "I am afraid any communication to the king would be intercepted."

Suggestion and counter-suggestion were offered and considered. Each was too risky or too apparent. Finally Mahrrah said, "I must go to the banquet." Her two stewards had never imagined such a thing could have entered Mahrrah's mind. Since Naaman had contracted leprosy she had refused to leave Jebel ed Ben.

The more she thought upon it the better she liked it. She would play upon the chamberlain's vanity. He would be bound to consider her presence there quite a feather in his cap. Mahrrah had given banquets of her own and she remembered quite well something unusual was always welcome.

"I will have a letter for you in just a few minutes." Mahrrah told the men. "I want both of you to ride to Damascus to deliver it and do not wait for an answer when you are sure the chamberlain has read it. Abu, you know where his house is, don't you?" Abu assured her he did. The men excused themselves and went to get the horses ready. In less than a half hour they were ready.

When they went back to the house, Mahrrah was ready with the scroll. It read, "Most Esteemed Chamberlain to Benhadad, King of Syria: It pleases me to know you are honoring our king by giving a banquet in his honor. He has been most benevolent to your humble servant in these times of distress.

"Sir Chamberlain, you would have no way of knowing to include me on your list of guests to the banquet, as I have done no traveling since my husband's affliction; however, my children are at the ages they can be left with the servants and I would consider it a double delight to be present at a banquet you are arranging and one that is given in honor of our great king. Because we are old friends, I know you will make a place for me at the banquet.

"It has been many months since I have seen our beloved king. It would be too great a surprise for him to see me at the banquet, knowing how closely I have stayed to Jebel ed Ben. I shall arrive at the palace one hour early. Please ask the king if he will see me for only a few moments so that my unexpected presence there will not detract from the festivities. Forgive the late hour of my request; I had not learned of the banquet until today.

"My servants need not wait for an answer. Hoping your banquet will be most successful, I am your humble servant. Mahrrah, wife of Naaman, Captain of the King's Hosts."

Mahrrah did not read the letter to the two men but handed it to Abu and bid them both goodbye with a warning to be careful.

9

he king's chamberlain had not thought of going to bed. He had just come from the palace and a late meeting with cooks and servants, making sure all was in readiness for the banquet now less than a full day away. The seating arrangement was exactly according to protocol, the most important guests closest to the king and the lesser important ones farthest away. Every detail was important and though he had given the responsibilities of those details to good and trusted men, he was not going to take any chances on a slip-up.

He had gotten the finest of everything. The decorations were colorful and promised to be displayed in new and clever ways. The food would be superb, prepared to perfection and served with grace and elegance. Entertainment was the finest available. The best of businessmen, architects and craftsmen had been invited and were commanded to bring their wives. True, some of the men had more than one wife, as was the custom in Syria at that time, but discretion compelled them to bring only one to the banquet.

The chamberlain sat at his desk going over the many lists. "Something else was needed," he thought. "I want everything that happens to impress the king. All preparations and plans can be excellent, but they can be commonplace without that touch of drama. But where is it? I cannot contrive the dramatic," he thought. "No, I dare not. That would be the quickest way to make the king very aware I was doing all to impress him and he would be aware then of nothing else. Perhaps that certain something will arise out of all we are having. That is all I can hope for, I suppose."

Presently a servant knocked at his chamber door. The chamberlain opened the door and his servant announced, "Two men are here from Jebel ed Ben, sir."

The chamberlain pondered the matter as he walked to the front door of his large house, "What kind of word would I be getting from the Lady Mahrrah?"

"Sir," Abu spoke up, "we are Abu and Joseph, stewards of the Lady Mahrrah, wife of Naaman,

Captain of the King's Hosts." The chamberlain acknowledged their greeting and Abu continued. "We have been commanded to give you this letter from our mistress."

The chamberlain took the scroll and Abu completed his explanation. "We were commanded to return when we knew the letter was safely in your hands, so if you will excuse us, sir, we will be leaving." With a low bow they were both gone.

The chamberlain read the letter with great interest. Then he grew excited about it as he considered its possibilities.

"There it is!" he discovered. "What could be more dramatic? Naaman's popularity had never waned in all the years he had served as head of the king's armies. Since it was found he was a leper and was still commanding those armies in spite of his dreadful disease, admiration for him had heightened. Had not the king given him every honor? Did a week pass that the king did not ask of his welfare and especially the welfare of his family? Had not the king provided the most envied house in all Syria for Naaman's wife and children? Indeed, the king had not ceased to seek new ways to compensate Mahrrah for the loss of her husband's companionship."

His diplomatic mind examined all the aspects of the matter and how he could best exploit it. He finally decided that when Mahrrah arrived at the palace he personally would escort her to the throne room. He knew there would be some rearranging to see to in the seating at the banquet, but well worth the trouble.

Mahrrah had risen early from a night of occasional sleep; not knowing how the chamberlain had taken her letter nor if he was part of the conspiracy kept her tossing half the night. Had she said all that was necessary in her letter? Surely the chamberlain would have to honor her request for a short audience with the king.

Abu and Joseph had returned at the time expected and had set about getting all done around the place that was necessary. Times were announced as to their departure and all equipment for Mahrrah's comfort was added to the cart. Joseph would drive the cart and Abu would follow on horseback; sometimes he would ride a few paces ahead, whatever conditions dictated.

Making sure everyone staying at Jebel ed Ben had their orders, Mahrrah, Abu and Joseph were soon on their way to Damascus and the great palace of Benhadad. The trip was quite uneventful and was completed in good time. Mahrrah had gauged the time precisely, arriving very near the time she·desired.

The chamberlain evidently had had servants

watching for Mahrrah's arrival and she was pleased with his gracious manner in receiving her. She was ushered to a spacious and comfortable library to await the king's summons. Abu and Joseph had seen her safely through the palace entrance and then had retired with the cart and horses to a place where they could see the entrance, in the event their services were needed.

The chamberlain had evidently told the king right away that Mahrrah was there and sought an audience with him. Benhadad did not keep her waiting. The chamberlain was soon back and beckoned Mahrrah to follow him. By this time she felt almost sure the chamberlain was not aware of what the coming evening promised, but she must remember to be on her guard. She could neither clear nor indict the chamberlain in the matter as she spoke to the king. He would know what to do and whom to trust.

"Your Majesty, The Lady Mahrrah, wife of Naaman, Captain of the King's Hosts!" the chamberlain announced.

Mahrrah bowed low. "Your Majesty!" she said. The king had already prepared for the banquet and was elegantly dressed. He assumed a paternal posture and smiled. His hands were slightly away from his side, palms outward in an imploring attitude.

"Dear Mahrrah!" said Benhadad, "Get up, my dear. What can I do for you? I was overjoyed when the chamberlain told me he had invited you to the banquet but had been keeping it a secret. I am delighted!" Then to the chamberlain, "Thank you. I shall send for you when we have concluded our visit."

"Your Majesty," Mahrrah began, "I'm afraid I invited myself to the banquet. The chamberlain no doubt would have asked me to come if he had any idea I would have, but I came more for this opportunity to speak to you than for the festivities. Are you certain we cannot be overheard?" She looked around the room.

At this the king's eyes narrowed. He had no idea what Mahrrah might be fixing to say, but he caught the serious tone in her voice and walked to the door and closed it.

"Now," said Benhadad, "I am certain. What is the matter?"

Mahrrah thought for awhile, weighing her words, then she spoke: "Your Majesty, I have come into possession of some information that leads me to believe your life is in danger and the good reputation of my husband is also in danger."

This news was startling to the king. "Madam," said Benhadad, taking on a more formal tone of voice, "how did you obtain this information? Can you give me names? Do you know of times or places?" The questions came fast and furiously, taking Mahrrah somewhat aback.

"Sir," assured Mahrrah, "I will tell you everything I know. Since I heard it, my only desire was to tell you about it. I knew you would know what to do."

Mahrrah told Benhadad exactly how she came to know of the plot, the names of the men from Aleppo, the caravan owners purported to be in back of it and the loyal merchants who uncovered it.

"I felt I was unable to trust anyone but you with this news," explained Mahrrah.

"And you were right, my dear," exclaimed the king. "There are times when the king cannot be certain who is loyal and who is not." Benhadad thought upon the matter for awhile, considering whether or not there was anything else he should ask Mahrrah. When he seemed assured he knew all he needed to know, he went to the door and asked a servant down the hall to summon the chamberlain. He soon came and escorted Mahrrah back to the library where she was to wait until a servant came to take her to the banquet hall.

Benhadad began removing his clothes. He had decided to wear something else now.

After he had finished dressing he went to the

door of his bed chamber and looked out. He was pleased to see an old man who had been in the palace since he was first made king. He called him to the chamber. The king had him come in and told him, "Do not let anyone see you do it, but quietly tell Roshek, my personal guard, to come to my chamber.

Presently the old servant appeared with Roshek. "Good," said the king. "Now, do the same thing four more times. I want you to go, one at a time to these men and bring each of them to me as you have Roshek." The king gave him the names and off went the servant to do as he was commanded.

10

he great hall could accommodate 500 sitting at banquet quite easily, leaving room for service and entertainment. The chamberlain had chosen all those attending with great care and they had all arrived with much pomp and fanfare, dressed expensively and colorfully; surely, all the tailors of Damascus and for that matter, every major city in Syria, had been occupied for weeks solely in fitting lord and lady for this moment. Indeed, one of the main enjoyments of the banquet, especially for the ladies, would be found in viewing the gowns of the other ladies, complimenting when close, criticizing when afar.

Brocades, silks, veils and embroideries, all bejeweled and sequinned with rare and costly gems, were worn as though balanced, mincing gingerly as they walked, never at ease.

The king and queen sat at the head table with the chamberlain and his wife and the main government officials and their wives on either side of them. They sat with their backs to the big wall opposite the windows. A small canopy jutted out from the wall ten feet above where the king and queen sat. Sweeping scalloped folds of satin were brought from it to frame this prominent place so the farthest diner could easily see where the king and queen sat.

Except for the ones sitting with the king, everyone was arranged so that they would face the king. Brilliant red bunting was draped and folded in front of the king's table with decorative cords and braids of blue and gold. The tables facing the king were similarly decorated but in a more simple fashion.

The chamberlain had arranged the seating so lady would be next to lady and gentleman would be next to gentleman, for the sake of conversation. The more important the diner, the closer he sat to the king.

After everyone had been seated, there was still a place left vacant, a place situated at the first table before the king and six or so places to his right. It caused quite a stir. "Who would dare fail to attend a banquet in honor of the king? Why hasn't the seating steward concealed the matter so it would not be so obvious to everyone?" But the chamberlain had so arranged that the seat be vacant until all were seated and then he had the chief steward escort Mahrrah to that seat. When everyone saw the king smiling at her so benevolently, they knew she must certainly be a very important person and very quickly, from table to table the news spread, "It is Mahrrah, Naaman's wife!"

A bit of time was allowed for all to whisper what they knew or didn't know of her and for those nearby to greet her and say how glad they were to see her. Soon, however, the trumpets signalled the beginning of the festivities. A loud voice introduced the Lord Chamberlain to the gathering and he arose.

"Esteemed and honored guests," the chamberlain called, slowly and distinctly. "It has been my happy privilege to invite you to this great banquet hall that you might assist me in honoring the conqueror of nations, the protector of the people and monarch of Syria, King Benhadad!" The room exploded with applause.

"Is he not responsible for peace with surrounding nations? Has he not guaranteed protection for the caravans traveling through this great land?" he continued. "Do not the merchants and craftsmen have first choice of goods going through our city from either direction? It is because of our great and noble ruler, Benhadad, King of Syria!"

The food was served by courses with constant filling of goblets with the fruit of the vine. Various tidbits were set for easy access so the diners could nibble and drink until the main courses were served. Various kinds of roast fowl were in abundance, as was lamb, beef and pork, all garlanded with lovely fruit and sauces. The songs of the musicians and the merry conversation of the celebrants afforded the delightful atmosphere that comes with combining elegance with familiarity and everyone basked in the knowledge they were part of history that night and would be able to recall it in the years to come to impress friend and loved one. Here were opportunities to make new acquaintances and remake old ones. The importance of this occasion would provide a bond for future transactions that would be valuable and profitable.

Benhadad knew them all, caravan owners, bazaar merchants, money-lenders, contractors and architects; all of them. His eyes flitted along the tables. His own table was slightly elevated so he could make out the farthest diners. He had met with them at some time or other in this very hall or in his private throne room. He could not recall all their names, but he could remember whether they were soldier or merchants, craftsman or money-lender. Every face was happy. That made him glad. The chamberlain had not spared a thing to make this a successful night. He was enjoying it, but he could have enjoyed it more had he not been given the evil tidings by Mahrrah only an hour before the banquet. But he had made preparations for any event, hasty though they were. He realized he must not appear uneasy or on his guard to any who would attempt to take his life lest they suspect their plans had been discovered. Benhadad wished to nip this matter in the bud tonight. So much was at stake!

He could not believe his chamberlain was part of the plot, but any intrigue was fraught with possibilities. He hoped he was not. He appreciated the great trouble he had gone to in arranging this banquet and for the clever way he had recognized Mahrrah. She had not been announced officially, but everyone soon knew she was there. Mahrrah looked good, brighter and more cheerful than he had ever seen her since it was found Naaman had leprosy.

The chamberlain had arranged the best in entertainment. The musicians were superb, playing flawlessly when there was no other feature and playing quietly in the background when the jugglers or acrobats or strong men performed, accentuating the drama and excitement of some particular part of their act with a roll on the drum or a clang of the cymbal when the act was successfully completed. He had had a special performing platform built that could be pushed to the place where all could see more easily and out of the way of the service traffic. Food and drink were constantly being brought to the banqueters.

Mahrrah had more time to look the entire hall over than had anyone else. She was really not expected to enter into very much conversation and indeed, she was careful on this point to not encourage very much talk that would detract from her vigil for the king's sake.

She did not wish to alarm the king unduly. She admired his demeanor, sitting there as though all was well. He never failed to keep his regal bearing.

After looking about her as much as she dared, and seeing nothing amiss among the diners, she began looking at all who were not guests: servers, acrobats, strong men, musicians; none missed her close scrutiny. All seemed intent on their duties. Everything seemed to be in order. She must be missing something. The men from Aleppo could not be hidden any place that she could not see. All draperies and partitions were well away from where the king sat and offered no permanent conceal-ment. No, they would have to be in plain view, a part of all the goings-on, unsuspected until it was time to strike. But where?

Mahrrah went back over everything she had seen. It was like being shown a face in the clouds; she was looking right at it, but it escaped her. She looked at everything once more, coming again to the orchestra.

"Let me see," she thought, "I have been looking at the orchestra as one; I must look at the musicians individually and watch them as they play. I dare not make be there what is not; but I must satisfy my mind thoroughly." The string portion of the band included four dulcimers and four zithers, but one of the zither players and one the dulcimer players did not have the flair for performing the others had. She looked longer and closer. They were picking or strumming the strings with the one hand, but not pressing the strings down with the other hand, as were their fellow bandsmen.

They might well be relatives of some of the musicians, smuggled into the orchestra so they might be able to enjoy the banquet and the other performers. She would observe them at length.

Presently the jugglers came back in. Mahrrah glanced their way, agitated they should interrupt her surveillance of the men in the orchestra.

Wait! These were not the same jugglers as before! Oh, she had no time to warn him! These men were clumsy; the others had been experts, but their clumsiness only served to bring laughter, not suspicion. The performing platform was situated at this time so Mahrrah could be seen by the king just beyond the jugglers. Was he looking only at them? Oh, he must look at her! He must!

Mahrrah waved her hand in front of her face, trying to be careful not to attract anyone else. Benhadad laughed and looked this way and that, then back at the jugglers.

"What's this? Mahrrah, just beyond the jugglers; is she trying to get my attention? She's frowning. I must not frown. I shall keep smiling and nodding. She is saying something silently with her lips. 'The jugglers! The jugglers!' Yes, that's what she is saying!"

Benhadad looked back again at the performance. He had been looking at their hands; now he looked at their faces. "Yes!" he thought, "I know those faces. I have seen them before. They are from Aleppo!"

"Guards!" cried Benhadad, "Sieze them!"

The king's preparation had paid off. Guards descended upon the assassins so suddenly they surprised completely the great audience as well as the hired killers. The Aleppo men had barely enough time to place their hands upon the large knives hidden in the folds of their garments, but the vice-like grip of the guards who first reached them, plus the hopelessness of their situation made them as meek as lambs. It was over very quickly. The king looked around and was pleased to see all exits well guarded.

Benhadad looked at his would-be assailants with a contemptuous smile. The great hall was as quiet as death. His eyes narrowed as he spoke. "You may save yourselves many unhappy hours in the hands of the tormentors if you point out any here who planned this deed against my person!"

The two men looked at each other, thinking over their plight, then they both turned toward two men seated just one table behind Mahrrah and to her right. They were Persians, perhaps the caravan owners of whom the loyal merchants wrote. The Persians stood up suddenly from their places and looked as though they wished to flee. Guards were upon them instantly and they were brought before the king. Benhadad surveyed them most solemnly. The Persians looked this way and that to avoid his gaze.

"Are there any more?" the king asked slowly and deliberately. "I will know the entire matter right now!"

"No, your majesty!" the Persians whined. "We are alone in this! We plead for mercy, your grace."

The countenance of Benhadad contained many things, but not one of them was mercy.

11

he unpleasant manner in which the assassins and the two Persians were questioned failed to reveal any others were involved in the plot to slay the king. When the king was sure all the facts were known, he had the conspirators hung from a high gallows in a public place as a warning to all.

Benhadad was pleased to find none of his cabinet or military staff were involved. The two fake musicians who had so taken up the attention of Mahrrah proved to be two guards the king himself had posted there so they would be in a better position to observe the crowd. They had not noticed the change of jugglers, and if Mahrrah had not warned the king, things could have gone differently. Two of the guards had bows at the ready with arrows set to strings. Had the assailants begun their attack the archers could have killed them and there might not have been the ample proof needed to clear up the matter in such short time.

The king had taken the precaution of putting on his mail armor and could have shielded the queen if the plotters had gotten too close.

Now, with things well in hand, Benhadad went to his favorite window overlooking Damascus and thought upon the last several days.

"That was a brave and unselfish thing the Lady Mahrrah did," he thought. "She had no way of knowing for sure I would even see her. She most certainly would be afraid someone in the palace was involved in the treachery. But this dear woman, in spite of all the heartache she has experienced, came here at such great risk to herself and warned me. The two Aleppo men were professional killers; they could have been successful and I could have already been entombed had I not been warned."

Benhadad went on with his ponderings. "What can I do for her? I feel so helpless because I am unable to give her what she wants the most: a well husband. Naaman has been reluctant to ride out to Jebel ed Ben lately. He says it serves no purpose but to upset Mahrrah, but I am so anxious that she know how I feel about Naaman and about her."

Thinking upon the matter for some time, a plan formed in Benhadad's mind. Orders were given to key men, who, in turn, gave orders to those under their command. Benhadad was going to give Mahrrah and her household a personal festival!

"Let's see," he mused, "I shall invite . . . no! Command! That's it. I shall command a few key government figures who feel toward Naaman and Mahrrah as I do to attend the festival. I shall have new awnings and canopies made and we shall have them erected on the grounds at Jebel ed Ben. I shall have several of the royal animals brought in cages for the children to see. All I invite will bring their families; Naaman's children see so little of other children."

Benhadad's mind was racing now. "Let's see. I shall need to send a message to Mahrrah saying I have a desire to use an area of her acreage for the purpose of entertaining some friends, including herself and family, on a particular day. That will make sure she stays home. We would not want the surprise to be too great. We shall have acrobats and musicians, jugglers and magicians. Ah, that's good! I shall find a special chariot, too, for Khalil. That little sister of his is big enough for her own pony now, too."

The day of the festival came and it was made to order. The sky was wondrously clear; a deep blue;

a slight breeze stirred the pleasant air and made the pennants flutter colorfully. The entire assembly of all those commanded to attend met at the palace to go in one group to Jebel ed Ben, nearly 200 people in all, counting attendants. Benhadad had gone over the list with the chamberlain and personally chose those he wished to attend. He set a limit to the number, often marking out some he might have otherwise included. Those finally left on the list remained on it because they had great admiration for Naaman and Mahrrah. Those in the entourage ranged from second to Naaman in the army to Patrol Leader Kurd and his wife.

It set Damascus buzzing. What was this? No word had come of a holiday. Why was the king on parade? The children along the route ran with the horses and carts until they were called back by their parents, and dogs barked their complaints against such unusual commotion.

Mahrrah only knew the king was bringing a group out to Jebel ed Ben to entertain them. The area was large enough to have most any kind of outdoor party and still afford such privacy the occasion might demand. Even though she was included, she had no idea the festivities were in her honor. The day the king wrote about came and found Jebel ed Ben sparkling and ready.

The servants of the estate had worked unusually

hard for several days; the men outside and the women inside. Mahrrah was not certain the king would even come into the house, but she was not taking any chances. If he did, he must see she had not treated his great gift but with the utmost respect.

Khalil was the first to hear it. He jumped on his pony and rode to the north road to look down the long incline. He had never seen so many people. He went rushing back to his mother to report what he had seen.

Benhadad had had trumpeters blow loud fanfares for several minutes after the merrymakers had begun the long climb up the north road so Jebel ed Ben would be aroused well in advance of their arrival. When they gained the summit, the family and servants were gathered to welcome them.

The king and queen lighted from their canopied carriage and gave proper greetings. Mahrrah was soon aware this entire affair was in her honor. She invited Benhadad and the queen into the house and soon they were all seated on the porch overlooking the Abana, the royal couple with Mahrrah and her children, watching the setting up of tents and canopies, booths and platforms. Of course Khalil could only temporarily be contained. Mahrrah was obliged to have Little One go bring

Joseph in for some special instructions concerning Khalil.

When Joseph came to the porch to see what Mahrrah needed, she introduced him to the king.

"Your highness," said Mahrrah, "this is Joseph, one of my stewards who was instrumental in saving your life."

Joseph bowed and said, "Your majesty." Joseph took note Mahrrah had used the word "steward" instead of "servant" or "slave."

"Joseph," observed the king, "it seems I am in your debt."

"Knowing your highness is safe is adequate payment," Joseph assured him.

"Thank you, Joseph," said Benhadad. "Nevertheless, I shall find some way of showing my appreciation."

Benhadad turned to Mahrrah. "Now, concerning young Khalil here, it may be he is in need of something special to keep him occupied while the tents are being erected." Then turning to Joseph he said, "With Lady Mahrrah's permission, take Khalil to the far side of the stables and you will find something I had fashioned for him."

Khalil was trembling with anticipation. He remembered the time the king surprised him with the pony and started to dart for the door, but Joseph sensed the king had not yet dismissed them so he held tightly to Khalil's wrist. Benhadad continued, "Djena, there is also something for you, too." The little girl was torn between remaining shy and dying of curiosity and following her brother and Joseph away from the royal company.

"All right," said Benhadad, grinning more broadly than usual, "off with you and see what I have brought you!"

Joseph bowed as well as he could while restraining Khalil and the three curious ones went out the door. The king chuckled, knowing what they would find and there followed explanations to Mahrrah and various exchanges of gratitude and grace.

It had been decided to arrange the equipment pertaining to the festival thirty paces or so in front of the house. There the yard had only a gradual slope going toward the river and the king could oversee all preparations. In just an hour or so everything was in readiness. The steward of such matters reported to the king and he invited Mahrrah to accompany him and the queen to the festival throne.

The festival steward had arranged everything well. The king and queen occupied a colorful central tent that had an unobstructed view of all the other tents and booths that made a semicircle from the throne tent to the right and to the left of it. The tents and booths for the musicians and exhibits to be enjoyed all day were left open, but the tents that housed the acrobats, magicians, strong men, jugglers and animal acts were left closed until it was their time to perform. The small audience was never quite sure which tent would open next and reveal some new and unusual act. Of course, this added to the excitement.

A bit down the hill on the western side of the semicircle the wild animals were kept. Benhadad made sure there was at least one of each animal the children might not have seen. There was a lion, a leopard, a bear, a baboon and a good many different kinds of monkeys.

On the eastern side of the semicircle and even closer to the river a kitchen had been set up with a large hole nearby in which red embers glowed and over which a fatted calf was roasting on a metal spit, turned slowly by one of the lesser cooks. Odors of the cooking food sometimes reached the revelers, promising good things to eat later on. The menagerie would get an occasional whiff too, and send up a roar.

Benhadad looked around him. The tents to his immediate right and left were filled with those he had invited. The sides of his tent and those containing his friends were left open so he could see them and they him. He received as much pleasure from watching their fun as from watching the performers. Khalil was charmed. He had reluctantly quit his chariot-racing to take his place beside Mahrrah as a spectator and Djena was just getting able to ride a bit without Joseph's assistance, but now they were both laughing and cheering with abandon. Mahrrah was delighted to see them having such fun. Little One was ever near to her to see to little Sabra's needs.

One would have thought the performers were doing their act in front of hundreds instead of the few on the hill overlooking the Abana River. The acrobats would burst from their tent with superb agility, bouncing, balancing, flipping, turning and jumping. The musicians knew just how to accentuate each trick with appropriate rolls on the drum and smashing of cymbals.

When the acrobats returned to their tent, trained dogs would come out to the platform barking and give a delightful performance; then a magician would come out and amaze the small crowd. After he and his attendant went back to their tent the acrobats would come back dressed as clowns and expertly fall and tumble. Khalil laughed at their antics and realized it took as much skill to perform the second act as the first.

Acrobats and magicians, jugglers and dogs all kept their audience spellbound for over an hour until word was finally given to the king the food was ready. Before long all were eating their fill. In fact, they were all so busy that only the guards on the crest of the north road were aware that two riders had come up the hill. They evidently knew them, but did not announce them. They silently saluted as they walked slowly out of the diner's view to an area west of the menagerie behind a canvas barrier.

The riders were Naaman and the king's physician.

12

redit for Syria's present freedom and greatness had gone to Naaman. He had risen through the ranks to the top of the Syrian Army. In battle he fought with skill and abandon; he seemed to have no fear and though he ascended in rank and leadership, he never failed to enter the fray, giving courage and strength to all who saw him in the thick of things. But he was a leper.

Naaman was a tall man. His disease had taken its toll on portions of his body, but it had not yet affected his tan, handsome face or his lustrous black hair streaked with silver. He looked a good bit older than his early thirties but he still sat tall in the saddle as he rode; he still surveyed all before him with practiced eye as one preparing for battle.

The man with Naaman was his own personal

physician, assigned to him by the king. His name was Jaichim. Jaichim had studied leprosy as no man alive ever had. Leprosy was his chief concern since he had been given this one famous patient to care for. No caravan traveled through Damascus that was not met by Jaichim. He examined new ointments and spices. Sometimes the caravan had a physician traveling with it from Persia or the Mediterranean, and Jaichim would sit by the hour with them discussing the merits of some particular herb or potion. On occasion he had access to an apothecary and would become enthused by its owner's claims and persuade Naaman to try a special salve. Naaman and Jaichim were constant companions. They were about the same age and had become the best of friends.

Jaichim had been in complete charge of this arrangement for Naaman to meet for awhile with Mahrrah. Even the direction of the wind had been taken into consideration so it would not blow from Naaman to Mahrrah carrying the disease from him to her. Certain distances were marked off and agreed to where Naaman and Mahrrah would stand. They would dismount and stand no closer than ten paces from each other. They dared not remain on their horses for fear one or both of the horses would bolt and get nearer. to each other than the prescribed distance.

"Lady Mahrrah," Benhadad had said to her, "I have a pleasant surprise for you now." The king leaned toward her in a very confidential manner as he continued. "Naaman is here at Jebel ed Ben."

Mahrrah had been so occupied with the festivities she hesitated a moment as if to get her mental bearings.

"Naaman?" she finally ventured. "Naaman, here?"

Benhadad waited for her various emotions to run their course. He sat and smiled, very pleased with himself, but he knew Mahrrah must be carefully made aware of the limitations and requirements attached to their meeting so he waited until he knew she would listen to all he had to say and would understand.

"When you see Naaman," Benhadad explained, "you will want to run to him and embrace him, but you must not. You must think of your own health as well as the health of your children. Jaichim, Naaman's physician is in complete control and will give you exact instructions by which you will safely meet. Do you understand?"

When the king was certain Mahrrah understood all the stipulations involved he took her to the back door of the house near the top of the north road and each mounted a horse and rode west far enough to remain out of sight of the guests. Soon they came to a large cedar that grew at the base of a hillock. Both would afford plenty of privacy for their rendezvous.

Twenty paces from the tree Benhadad said, "We'll dismount here. Now remember," he stressed as he stepped down from his horse, "you must obey the physician without question, is that clear?"

"Yes, your majesty," said Mahrrah excitedly. "Please take me to Naaman now!"

The king took Mahrrah by the arm and they walked beneath the great cedar and stopped in its shade.

Jaichim appeared from around the southwest bend of the small hill. "Greetings, Lady Mahrrah!" he called. "That is a good place for you to stand. You will notice I have arranged some rocks two paces toward me. You may come no closer than those rocks."

"All right, Jaichim," Mahrrah answered, "I understand."

Soon Naaman came into view and the king and physician withdrew to leave the couple alone.

A gentle breeze blew from back of Mahrrah's right shoulder, blowing her dark hair to her left and a bit toward Naaman. For several moments they stood and looked at one another. This was the first time they had been this close since it was discovered Naaman had leprosy. They both thought how fortunate it was they had been carefully warned to stay in a particular area; the temptation was so great to run to each other's arms.

"Dear Mahrrah," Naaman broke the silence; "you look very well; beautiful, in fact. How are the children?"

Mahrrah was relieved at Naaman's unemotional conversation. It served to steady her.

"They are fine, my husband," she said. "And you are looking well too."

"Yes," Naaman assured her, "Jaichim is the best doctor in Syria and he declares I am the healthiest leper in the world." Naaman's easy humor put Mahrrah at ease and before long she launched into light and cheerful accounts of the children and all their childish sayings and doings.

"The king has told me of your involvement in saving his life," Naaman said. "The king's safety used to be part of my duties. Are you after my job?"

"No," Mahrrah laughed, "I want no more of that sort of thing. I was petrified!" And they both laughed.

Mahrrah told Naaman all about Little One and how she had brightened up Jebel ed Ben and the dramatic reunion of Little One and her brother.

She went into detail concerning Joseph's part in foiling the plot. Naaman laughed when she told him how Kurd had outfitted Little One at the merchants' expense.

"Yes!" Naaman declared, "I've been watching that man and I believe he is due a promotion. It is good to have so many good friends, isn't it?" And Mahrrah agreed. "It seems you are in good hands, dear wife." Naaman went on. "Let us not despair. If there is a cure for this terrible disease, Jaichim will surely find it. We are far better off than the poor lepers who huddle in caves and wander in the wilderness, fed only by the garbage of more fortunate people. I do what I can for them."

Naaman's change in conversation encouraged Mahrrah to speak freely.

"Oh yes, my husband!" she declared, "I know we are so well-off compared to so many." Then her voice broke. "I didn't want to cry," Mahrrah sobbed, "because I know it makes you sad and I don't want you to remember me this way. You are right. We must not give up hope. I shall always hope, dear one. I shall always hope!"

Naaman remained silent for awhile, wishing he had not spoken of his plague. How he longed to rush to Mahrrah's side and comfort her with his arms about her and her head on his shoulder, but he stood in his appointed place, helpless.

"Are you going to be all right?" he finally asked.

"Yes, but I must be getting back to the children. They will be wondering where I am." Mahrrah spoke in a good strong voice, giving Naaman the assurance he needed.

The two stood for a time looking at each other as if they sought to imprint a lasting picture on their minds to have for comfort in days to come.

"Jaichim!" Naaman called loudly, "We are ready."

Benhadad and Jaichim came from the direction of the house and took their charges in hand. The king and Mahrrah waved good-bye to Naaman and Jaichim and stood watching until they rode out of sight toward the north road.

As they mounted their own horses Mahrrah spoke to the king. "Thank you, your highness. The day has been full of surprises and excitement, but seeing Naaman again has been the most precious happening possible. Thank you so much!" Benhadad knew he need not speak as Mahrrah brushed her tears away. He just smiled. Mahrrah was happy and that made him glad.

13

fter the entertainment and the dinner, the balance of the afternoon was given to looking at interesting things in the makeshift bazaar and making a purchase now and then. Too, the menagerie was very appealing to all the children present. Adults were always close at hand to see that the children didn't get too close to the dangerous animals.

By the time Benhadad and Mahrrah returned to the site, a good number of the tents and canopies were being rolled up and loaded on the wagons and animals to carry back to Damascus. Friends were saying good-byes to friends and some families had started down the long hill toward the city.

Mahrrah excused herself and went into the house. The king and queen bid the merrymakers farewell and received their thanks for the festival. The festival steward stayed busy checking every detail entailed in dismantling everything and leaving the grounds in the tidy condition in which they were found.

Little One had the promises of Khalil and Djena that they would stay near the king and queen and wave good-bye to all the people as they left and would come into the house as soon as everyone had gone.

Sabra was tuckered out and Little One had only to put him on the bed and cover him up and she was able to see if she could assist Mahrrah.

The door to Mahrrah's chamber was open but Little One knocked. "Come in," said Mahrrah softly. When Little One went in, Gherza, Abu's wife, was standing near Mahrrah looking at her as Mahrrah sat weeping. Little One looked uneasily from one to the other, fearing she had entered upon something that did not concern her; however, she was not sent away, so she went to where Mahrrah sat.

"What is the matter, dear lady?" Little One asked sincerely. Gherza knew Mahrrah was too overcome with emotion to speak, so she explained, "Madam has just come from seeing her husband and she longs to see him made well."

Little One knelt at Mahrrah's feet and wept too. Gherza was touched by Little One's honest sympathy and she also wept. Finally, Little One sighed thoughtfully, "Would God my lord Naaman were with the prophet that is in Samaria! for he would recover him of his leprosy."

Mahrrah took her hands away from her eyes and looked at Little One's face pressing against her knee. Gherza looked on in disbelief. "What did you say, child?" Mahrrah asked.

"I said, dear mistress, would God my lord were with the prophet that is in Samaria, for he would recover him of his leprosy."

Mahrrah looked deeply into Little One's eyes as she held her face in both her hands. She could see nothing there but love—love, sympathy and honesty.

"There is hope?" Mahrrah asked timorously, barely daring to hope. "There is hope, Little One?"

"Yes," answered Little One, "in Israel."

Now there were tears of hope in Mahrrah's eyes and she turned to the older maid, "Gherza!" But Gherza had left the room.

Gherza found Abu, her husband, near the king's carriage.

The king and queen were preparing to leave. Benhadad knew Mahrrah would not feel up to seeing them off and he congratulated Abu on his care of Mahrrah and her family and his ability in overseeing the affairs at Jebel ed Ben.

"Abu, I know of your part in warning me of the

plot on my life and I am seeking a reward appropriate for you," said the king.

Abu bowed low. "Your good health is ample reward, sir." On rising, Abu saw Gherza and the anxious look on her face. "Excuse me, your highess; something may be wrong." Benhadad waited to see what troubled Gherza. She was too timid to speak to the king or even look at him, but she told Abu softly and excitedly all she had overheard in Mahrrah's room.

"Gherza, are you certain." Abu did not want to raise the king's hopes if there was the slightest doubt in what Little One had said.

"Yes, I am certain." Gherza used Abu's very word to emphasize how sure she was. "I have never known Little One to ever come close to lying. If she says Naaman can be cured in Samaria, it must be so."

Abu was stunned. He was not quite sure what to say. The king was waiting. It was like translating from Persian to Hebrew and then back again; he sought to couch his words in exact phrases.

"Your excellency," Abu began, "you know of the maid that is from Israel who is called Little One. She is the sister of Joseph, who first learned of the plot against your life."

"Yes, yes! What is it, man?" Benhadad was impatient.

"The maid of Israel says there is a prophet in Samaria that can recover our lord Naaman of his leprosy." There! He had said it. Abu hadn't believed it, but he was almost forced to tell it, by wife and king. His voice had trailed off so Benhadad was obliged to lean forward to get the words.

"What did you say, man! Speak up! It sounded like you said there was a cure for Naaman in Samaria," the king roared.

"Yes, sir! That is what the maid of Israel said," Abu affirmed. "But she is a slave. Why would she want her master cured?" asked the king.

"Because she loves him," Abu said simply.

"She has never seen Naaman; why should she love him?" asked Benhadad.

"She loves everybody, sir," explained Abu, certain the king wouldn't believe that either. "Her integrity is never questioned, your highness," he said, a bit more confident.

Benhadad turned in his carriage and looked at his wife. Then he looked at Abu and then Gherza, then back to Abu and again to the queen. He was speechless, but he had declared many times that he would explore any avenue of hope wherever it might be.

"All right!" he bellowed, "That settles it!" Then to the driver of his carriage, "Call for a courier!"

The voice of the driver rang out for the courier who appeared almost immediately. The man dismounted from his horse and bowed low. "Your Majesty."

"Yes. Take this message to Jaichim, Naaman's physician immediately. He is to meet me at the palace right away. He is not to delay. If you hurry, he should reach the palace about the same time I do." The second the messenger sensed the king was finished with his orders, he was in the saddle and gone.

Abu and Gherza stood with their hands bowed respectfully. As soon as the courier had left, the king looked about him to make sure there was nothing more he should do before leaving Jebel ed Ben. A smile crossed his face as he looked beyond Abu and Gherza at Mahrrah standing on the back porch with an arm around Little One. Mahrrah's face was dazzling with hope as Little One looked up at her. Mahrrah waved to the king and queen.

"It is a bright day, Lady Mahrrah!" the king called to her. "The sun will not be well risen before your husband is on his way to see the prophet that is in Samaria!" He motioned to his steward and the royal entourage was soon on its way back to the palace.

14

enhadad found Jaichim waiting for him when he arrived at the palace in Damascus. The king lost no time with formalities. He quickly summoned Jaichim to his quarters and spoke to him firmly.

"There is deliverance for Naaman in Samaria," he said. Jaichim was stunned; too stunned, in fact, to answer. The king continued, "I have been told by the most reliable source that there is a prophet in Samaria who can recover Naaman of his disease."

Jaichim thought it best to hold his peace and let the king do whatever pleased him. He was somewhat dubious of there being any hope in Samaria, but if the king had reason enough to pursue the matter, who was he, a mere physician, to dissuade him?

"You must arrange a caravan to go to Samaria,"

Benhadad explained. "I don't know exactly where this prophet resides, but I will write a letter to the king of Israel and he will direct you to the prophet. Get everything in readiness. I shall have the chamberlain draw up the necessary papers so that you may receive ample gold and silver from the treasury. I don't know how much this mystic might charge for his services. You had better take ten changes of raiment also."

Jaichim could only mutter "yes, Sirs" and go along with the idea, but he failed to see how some religious fanatic was going to cure Naaman of the world's worst disease.

Enough men were placed at Jaichim's disposal to make the preparations necessary for the journey in the shortest amount of time. When all the orders had been given and his list of requirements doubly checked, Jaichim hastened to report back to Naaman.

From the palace back to Naaman's command quarters, Jaichim thought of what he might say to Naaman; how he would phrase the matter. He pondered, "Naaman will probably be as dubious about this matter as I am. How many hours have the two of us conversed about this dreadful plague? I have questioned him constantly about how it felt and when we tried a new remedy, I would ask him about his reaction to it."

It was true. The two friends had formed a campaign against the disease. Naaman called it "The Jaichim Campaign."

Sure enough, Naaman was adamant. "What?" he roared, "Travel all the way to Samaria to see some holy man? Why, it's absolutely the silliest thing I ever heard of!"

Jaichim let him fume. He had often seen the great man like this. All remedies were silly to Naaman, as useless as mud in the streets, but Jaichim found that when he let him vent his emotions for awhile, he would simmer down and become reasonable. Of course, they both knew they would leave at dawn. The journey had been ordered by the king. The caravan would come by the command post just before dawn and Naaman and Jaichim would go out and board their appointed camel and away they would go to Samaria. The king had ordered it. They would obey.

The steward of the caravan handed Benhadad's letter to the king of Israel to Jaichim and Jaichim put it with his personal effects where he could easily get to it at journey's end.

It was Jaichim's first trip to Samaria. He had accompanied a caravan east to Persia seeking a particular powder used by lepers near Shushan the palace. Some slight improvement had been noted in the condition of other lepers and Jaichim brought it back to Damascus, but it had not helped Naaman.

Naaman had been to Samaria on several campaigns. He had never liked it and said so.

"Compare, if you will the two countries," he said to Jaichim. "Where are the crystal-clear mountain streams or the gentle slopes descending to verdant valleys? Who would want to live in such a place? It is rocky and barren, an absolute wilderness!" On and on he raved as Jaichim smiled and turned his face away from his friend. The differences between the two countries were not all that pronounced. True, there were differences, but Samaria had its places of beauty just as Syria had its places of desert.

They lacked for nothing on the journey. There was ample food and drink, and plenty of guards rode near the caravan providing the best of protection.

Word of its coming had already preceeded the caravan. The number of its guards and the burdens of the camels gave some idea of its importance. Jehoram, king of Israel, thought it best to simply wait in his palace in Samaria and see what the caravan brought, good news or bad, rather than send an emissary to inquire of it. If it were good news, he could wait awhile; if it were bad news, why hurry it?

King Jehoram had his father's penchant for trifles. He deplored such interruptions of his solitude and looked upon them as possible threats to his throne. He was as petulant as his father Ahab and as demanding as his mother Jezebel.

The caravan made camp outside the walls to the city. Jaichim and the caravan steward rode with two of the armed guards into the city, stopping at the gate long enough to say they were on an errand of great importance and were on their way to the palace to seek an audience with King Jehoram. Then they rode slowly to the palace allowing ample time for news of their arrival to precede them.

Sure enough, when they reached the palace entrance, its doors came open and an honor guard comprised of two soldiers and a diplomat met them.

"Sirs!" said the diplomat, "We have just now learned of your coming to Samaria. Can we be of any service to you?"

"Yes," replied Jaichim, endeavoring to be as formal as the diplomat had been, "we have a letter from Benhadad, King of Syria, to Jehoram, King of Israel. We are commanded to deliver it personally."

"Certainly, sirs. Will you wait until I return?" Without waiting for an answer, the diplomat disappeared into the palace leaving the two soldiers with the visitors. Very soon he was back and asked Jaichim and the caravan steward to follow him into the palace. The two men dismounted and followed the diplomat to the king's throne room.

The diplomat went directly into the throne room where Jehoram sat upon his throne. He stopped five paces in front of the throne and bowed. When he was erect again he said quite loudly, "Your majesty, these two men have a message to you from the king of Syria."

"Give me the message," said Jehoram.

Jaichim walked directly up to the throne and with a respectful bow handed Benhadad's letter to the king of Israel. The letter read, "Now, when this letter is come unto thee, behold, I have therewith sent Naaman my servant unto thee that thou mayest recover him of his leprosy."

Jehoram looked up from the letter. "Which of you is Naaman?" he asked.

"Neither of us, your highness," said Jaichim. "We thought it would be best to leave the king's servant outside the city wall, seeing he is a leper."

"You thought correctly," observed Jehoram, "but I do not understand this letter." Jehoram tried to contain himself in front of these strangers, but he could not. His worst fears were being realized. The king of Syria was trying to start war with Israel. Again he read the letter and got up from his throne.

It was impossible to control his frustration. Jehoram began tearing his clothes and crying loudly, "Am I God, to kill and to make alive that this man doth sent unto me to recover a man of his leprosy? Wherefore consider, I pray you, and see how he seeketh a quarrel against me."

Jaichim considered nothing of the sort, but he would not dare tell Jehoram so. In fact, he was not about to tell the king of Israel anything at all at this point; anyone could see this man, though a king, was utterly beside himself with fear and rage. The diplomat seemed to think silence was very appropriate at the moment, so Jaichim thought it must also be the most diplomatic. Too, it appeared the best posture was to stand quietly and look at the floor.

Jehoram raged on and on, cursing his birth, his plight, his throne, his lot in life, his people, his enemies and the world in general. The diplomat bowed low and retreated five more steps so the king might have ample room in which to rage. The caravan steward and Jaichim took that to mean they should also move farther away from the king and gratefully complied, bowing and retreating.

After some thirty minutes' duration of royal

raging, some action at the door to the throne room
caught the diplomat's attention and he bowed very
low and withdrew to the door where he was handed
another letter to the king. After pondering the
king's mood a few moments, as his vocation often
required him to do, the diplomat concluded
Jehoram had become as tired of his harangue as
his listeners and would welcome some interruption
to it, so he walked to within five paces of the king
and stopped, bowing low.

Jehoram took a deep breath and ascended his
throne again. "Yes, what is it now?" he asked with
a mixture of relief and agitation.

"Your highness, there is another letter for you."
explained the diplomat. Jehoram considered the
whole world had seen his tantrum; there was no
longer any reason to be secretive. "Well, read it,
man! Who sent it?" he blurted.

"It is from Elisha, the man of God, sir,"
answered the diplomat. "The letter says, 'Wherefore hast thou rent thy clothes? Let him come now
to me, and he shall know that there is a prophet in
Israel'."

The diplomat knew well what would ensue. He
knew Jehoram was glad the leper was taken off his
hands but he had to be extremely angry that
someone outside the palace knew of his garment-
tearing tantrum, so he knew Jehoram would order

all of them to leave but would not do so in a gentle manner.

"Out!" screamed Jehoram. "Out! Out! All of you!" he screamed as shrilly as his mother Jezebel might have screamed. "Get out of my sight! Take them to that old hermit! Out! Out!"

The three men rushed quickly out of the throne room midst various threats of beheadings and burnings, thankful to be away from such anger.

The diplomat ordered a horse, and he rose with Jaichim, the steward and the two guards back to the caravan. When the group was well away from the palace, Jaichim turned to the diplomat who was smiling at something only he knew. "I do not understand. Who told Elisha about the king's fit?" he asked.

Jaichim's question unleashed a flood of mirth from the diplomat. "That is the point of the matter, my friend," said the ambassador. "Elisha lives a good hour's ride from the palace. He had to send that message before the king had even gotten the letter from your king."

Jaichim was stunned and his look of disbelief sent the diplomat into fresh fits of laughter, tears streaming down his face. Jaichim thought this too good to keep, so he told it to the steward and he was as shocked as Jaichim had been.

Seeing the look on the steward's face, Jaichim

realized how funny he must have appeared to the diplomat and soon he was laughing as loudly as the diplomat. The steward happily told the soldiers and soon there was a quartet of mad men on their way to the caravan.

It took a good while for the laughter to subside, but all it took to revive it was a smile or a jesture or phrase from Elisha's letter.

"Ah!" cried the diplomat, "I can't remember when I last enjoyed such laughter. There is too little to laugh at in Samaria these days."

Jaichim pondered the matter at length. "What kind of mystical creature is this Elisha that he can tell the future? Whatever he is, he cannot be dull."

15

lisha's house personified simplicity. It was as rustic and weather-beaten as its main occupant. The little log house was situated where tree and earth and stone converged in a harsh ravine that would have been easily overlooked had not someone pointed it out. The clearing in front of the house was comprised of huge flat stones, that could have been mistaken for the courtyard of an ancient ruin. Grass and weeds grew from the soil in the borders of the rocks and the prophet's donkey munched, unstaked, the tender plants.

The River Jordan was a good mile away and could be seen on a clear day from the slightly elevated site of the prophet's house. It had a simple entrance. The windows were simple openings, more for looking at the stars than the world.

How great as the contrast when the Syrian

general's caravan paraded elegantly and regally before the prophet's home! Naaman knew the value of first impressions and had had his guards wear full battle armor, helmets plumed and shining. His own chariot was gleaming, pulled by two white horses, exactly alike. Ensigns and banners fluttered from every fourth soldier. What splendor! What dash! What show! It was all utterly wasted on Elisha.

Before any announcement could be made that the great Naaman had arrived, Elisha's servant appeared at the front door and closed it behind him.

"Are you Elisha?" Jaichim asked.

"No," the servant answered. "I am Gehazi, his servant."

"Please tell your master that Naaman, Captain of the Host of King Benhadad of Syria is out here and desires to be healed of his leprosy." Jaichim thought the servant would hasten back inside the house.

"Which one is Naaman?" Gehazi asked.

"The man in the chariot," Jaichim answered.

Gehazi walked over to the chariot and looked at Naaman. "The man of God says for you to go and wash in Jordan seven times and thy flesh shall come again to thee and thou shalt be clean."

Naaman was incensed. Taking up the reins to

his horses he cracked his whip over them angrily and drove recklessly around the outer edge of the clearing. Jaichim waited for Naaman to simmer down. He finally brought his chariot to a halt directly before the door of the small house and said loudly, wanting Elisha to hear, "Behold, I thought he will surely come out to me and stand and call on the name of the Lord His God and strike his hand over the place and recover the leper. Are not Abana and Pharpar, rivers of Damascus better than all the waters of Israel? May I not wash in them and be clean?" So he turned and went away in a rage.

Jaichim went over to the steward of the caravan and spoke briefly with him. "You must help me persuade Naaman to follow the instructions of this man. I cannot help but believe he may be helped. We have come this far. How can it hurt?" The steward agreed and they both walked over to where Naaman had once more stopped his chariot.

The steward spoke to him most reverently. "My father," he said to Naaman, "if the prophet had bid thee do some great thing, wouldest thou not have done it? How much rather then when he said to thee, 'Wash and be clean'?"

Naaman was visibly moved by his steward's logic. Resolutely, he gave crisp orders. "Let the guards stay with the camels. You and Jaichim ride alongside my chariot to the river." The two men gleefully ran to their horses and went with Naaman. As an after thought he called back to his steward, "Invite the diplomat to come too." And Jehoram's ambassador ran quickly to his horse and caught up with the trio.

The river was swollen from recent rains and muddy. Naaman nearly lost his boots in the slippery bog as he sought to get out into a depth of water that would cover him. He looked back toward the band where his companions stood by their horses. They all nodded encouragement.

"Seven times, he said?" Naaman called.

"Seven times!" called back his physician. And Naaman disappeared beneath the surface of the muddy water. All three on the shore counted aloud at the great man's washings. And Naaman counted too.

As Naaman came up the seventh time he brushed the hair and water from his eyes and began walking toward his friends, tearing away his upper garments as he went, looking intently at his chest and shoulders, stumbling because he was not careful to watch his steps.

"Jaichim!" he cried, "Look at me, physician! I'm clean! I'm clean! Jaichim!" he screamed, "Look at my flesh! Is it not new?"

Jaichim went toward his patient and they met

and floundered joyously in the mud together. When they both came to shore, Jaichim pulled away other portions of Naaman's garments where leprosy had been raging and they rejoiced together to see pink healthy flesh like a baby's where once there had been the white, unyielding scales of leprosy. Shouts of joy accompanied each new discovery and the four men embraced in celebration.

"Amazing!" said the diplomat.

"Unbelievable!" cried the steward.

"Phenomenal!" glowed the physician.

"It is a miracle of God!" said Naaman.

A quiet elation fell upon the quartet when they realized this miracle would not be snatched from them and they would have the rest of their lives to reflect upon it. They exulted in being present to see it.

"I shall not ride. I rode my chariot up to the prophet's house like a pompous conqueror. I wonder that he did not turn me away. Let us walk back up and stand before the man of God and declare what his God has done." And he returned to the man of God, he and all his company, and came and stood before him and said, "Behold, now I know that there is no God in all the earth but in Israel: now therefore, I pray thee, take a blessing of thy servant."

But Elisha said, "As the Lord liveth, before Whom I stand, I will receive none."

Naaman urged Elisha to take it, but he refused.

Then Naaman said, "Shall there not then, I pray thee, be given to me two mules' burden of earth? For I will henceforth offer neither burnt-offering nor sacrifice unto other gods, but unto the Lord." Elisha enjoyed Naaman's resolution.

Everyone's attention was fastened on the leathery-faced prophet before whom they stood, studying his deepset eyes and shaggy brows. They looked at his coarse robe and gnarled staff, a poor man, rejecting a fortune. Elisha stood patiently, listening to Naaman.

"In this thing the Lord pardon me, that when my master goeth into the house of Rimmon to worship there, and he leaneth on my hand, and I bow myself in the house of Rimmon: the Lord pardon thy servant in this thing." Naaman was completely humbled; all present could tell.

"Go in peace," Elisha said to him. So Naaman and his entourage began going back to where they had camped so they might prepare to return to Damascus. But Gehazi, the servant of Elisha, caught up with the host of Syrians and led them to believe Elisha had changed his mind about receiving gifts from them. He asked and received from Naaman two talents of silver and two changes of garments and hid them.

When Gehazi returned to Elisha, Elisha asked him, "Where have you been, Gehazi?"

"I've been no place," Gehazi lied.

Elisha looked at his servant intently.

"Went not mine heart with thee, when the man turned again from his chariot to meet thee? Is it time to receive money and to receive garments, and oliveyards, and vineyards, and sheep, and oxen, and manservants, and maidservants? The leprosy therefore of Naaman shall cleave unto thee, and unto thy seed for ever."

And Gehazi went out from Elisha's presence a leper as white as snow.

aaman and his host went happily on their way back to Damascus, oblivious of Gehazi's deceit and judgment. At the camp site in Samaria it was decided Naaman and Jaichim would take six of the guards with them and a change of horses with ample provision and ride on to Damascus. Without waiting for the slow-moving caravan they could reach home in less than half the four days the trip down had taken. For the first time since he had taken leprosy Naaman felt like a warrior in the ranks, a reckless stripling, ready to take on a company of troops by himself.

Life was a lark. All was new. The land of Samaria was beautiful. In their hard ride for home Naaman would come upon a country scene with sheep and shepherds framed by meadow and mountain, a brook running nearby. It was a common enough scene, but Naaman could not help but rein up and stand for moments to gaze upon it in wonder. "Look!" he would say, "Have you ever seen anything as breathtaking?" Most of the time Jaichim could not really see what Naaman pointed out, but he could see the glow on Naaman's face and that was more than satisfying to him.

Naaman sometimes broke into song. He would sing soldier songs and make the guards join in. If it happened he had by accident chosen a song he had forgotten was rather earthy, he would stop and cry out, "No! that is not a good song to sing. Those are not good words. I am a family man! Let us sing another song." And then he would launch into a ballad he knew was safe.

Their last night on the trail they chose a camp site near a lovely stream situated where there was ample protection against surprise. It would be hard to get to sleep; tomorrow was going to be a day much longed for, but they must try.

After their supper of meal cakes and brush rabbit, Naaman turned to the six soldiers that had escorted him and Jaichim. "Which of you feels up to sacrificing a night's sleep to ride ahead and tell the king and my family we are this near home?" They all volunteered immediately and began arguing why they were best suited to ride and give the word.

This struck Naaman very funny and he burst into laughter. "Here I was worried we should have to cast lots to see who would go. Now I find we must cast lots to see who will get to go." One of the young men was finally chosen; he picked out the freshest horse, made sure he had plenty of water and rode for home.

* * * * * * * *

Benhadad had placed trumpeters a half-mile apart five miles out from Damascus. If a rider came from the caravan, the trumpeter fartherest from the city would call, "Is Naaman delivered?" and if the rider answered, "Naaman is delivered!" the trumpeter would blow his trumpet continuously in great long blasts and the next trumpeter toward the city would take up the signal and blow continually and so on, until the signal had reached the ears of the king. However, if the answer was, "Naaman is not delivered," the first trumpeter would blow two single blasts from the trumpet and no more.

The chosen soldier had ridden the entire night, slowing only to rest his horse. When the first rays of the sun showed on Mount Hermon, the rider reached the first trumpeter. A soldier was posted to make sure the rider stopped for the question,

"Are you from Naaman's caravan?" The rider saw the soldier and recognized him and brought his horse to a stop only two paces from him. He was about to answer the soldier's question when the impatient trumpeter forty feet above them on a boulder cried impatiently, "Is Naaman delivered?"

The rider gladly answered loudly, and unmistakably, "Naaman is delivered!" The trumpeter blew such continued notes on the instrument one could tell he felt he was born for that moment. How joyous! How blessed! What bountiful news! Even the trumpet seemed alive!

By the time the rider got to the second trumpeter he had guessed the system and knew the good news had preceeded him, but he knew too the king would be anxious to listen to an exact account of just how Naaman was delivered. He rode his horse unmercifully the last five miles to the city gates.

Benhadad had sent soldiers and servants out to Jebel ed Ben; the servants to stay on and tend the house and stock and the soldiers to bring Mahrrah and her family and servants to the palace where they had spent the last three days and nights waiting word from the caravan. The king had explained his system with the trumpets, so everyone stayed in constant readiness to hear their sound.

Khalil heard it first. "Mother!" he cried. "Listen to the trumpets! The valley is filled with their sounds!"

Mahrrah had not yet risen. She sat up, startled. "What? Khalil? Are you sure?" Mahrrah said.

"Yes, I'm sure! Listen!" With great restraint Khalil kept quiet so Mahrrah could hear the trumpets.

Mahrrah listened. Trumpeters on the wall had already taken up the signal and continued the clarion notes in brass.

She grabbed Khalil and hugged him and wept. "We have him back, Khalil! We have him back!" When Khalil could get away, he gaily woke up Djena and Sabra, making them listen to the trumpets.

Little One ran to Mahrrah and embraced her joyously. "Thank God!" she murmured.

"Yes!" agreed Mahrrah, "Thank God!"

Benhadad soon knocked at the door. "Listen to the trumpets!" he called through the door to Mahrrah, "Hear the trumpets?"

Mahrrah, Little One and the children were soon dressed and found the king out in the hall anxious to rejoice with them.

Benhadad soon discovered his symphony of trumpets had served to awaken the whole city of Damascus. It suddenly occurred to him he must get soldiers to keep the throng back from the gates to the city or his hero would not be able to get to the palace. Orders were given. "Keep the streets open so Naaman can ride in them, but let the populace celebrate his return. It has been so long since they have seen him."

"Ah, good!" grinned Benhadad, rubbing his hands, "We shall have a parade. I shall go to the city gates and ride back to the palace with Naaman."

The rider from Naaman's small group had arrived and told all to the king. He was incredulous. "You don't mean it. In a muddy river named Jordan, you say! I have never heard of such a thing!"

The young rider was in his glory. He had the undivided attention of the king. He told the king where Naaman had camped and the king calculated quite accurately when they would be arriving. Preparations were made to receive the hero and his escorts. As a partial reward, Benhadad asked the courier to accompany him to the gate.

The king had his own chariot brought for Naaman to ride in, the horses led by strong men so Naaman would have nothing to do but return the waves of the crowd. Word was passed: bring flowers and fronds. Important government officials were notified to be present at the gates with the king. Military men closest to Naaman formed an honor guard and planned to lead their horses before Naaman's chariot so they would not be higher than he in the parade.

Mahrrah and her household waited at the palace. Neither she nor the king wished her reunion with Naaman to be public. He was a public figure, true; and the public would have their time with him, but when the cheering ceased, he would come to his beloved Mahrrah, privately.

Little One had slipped away for a few minutes to be alone. She went quietly down to where she had slept the last three nights and knelt by the little cot.

"Dear Lord," she prayed, "thank you for letting me come to live with Mahrrah and her family because they needed to know about the prophet in Israel and I know you put me here to tell them. Thank You for the love You put in my heart for them so I would want to tell them about You. Whatever You have in store for me, dear Lord, please give me the words I should say to everyone and the love for them I need so they will believe me. Amen."

17

fter her prayer, Little One went back to take her place with Mahrrah on the palace wall. The parade would be coming soon. They would be able to watch its progress all the way from the city gates. The entire household from Jebel ed Ben was with Mahrrah and her family. Only Mahrrah and Abu had seen such crowds before. Little One and Mahrrah's two older children were enthralled by the ebb and flow of the growing throng, all of them vying for a vantage point from which to see the parade. Soldiers were kept busy trying to keep some sort of order, but they were as much in the mood for celebration as the mob they were trying to control; after all, their famous leader was soon to make his appearance and it was reported he was free from his loathsome disease.

Presently, some soldiers opened the doors to the

palace parapets behind Mahrrah and her group, and three gentlemen were added to the watchers: Wadi, Twafik and Butros, the merchants of the bazaar. They were enchanted with the entire affair. Recognizing Mahrrah, Abu and Little One they bowed very low, and with a grin that made their eyes disappear, they all began talking at once.

"The Lady Mahrrah! Abu, trusted steward! Yes! And Little One, precious jewel from Israel! The king himself sent for us and had us brought here so we might better see the parade. We were not told you would be here. How delightful! What a marvelous surprise! Lady Mahrrah, you must be beside yourself with impatience to see your husband! It is such a moment we have long prayed for!" All was said excitedly, loudly and simultaneously, but Mahrrah was amused and delighted. All she could say was, "Yes! Oh, yes!" over and over.

Suddenly, even above the din of the mob below them a trumpet could be heard coming from the direction of Samaria. It kept sounding. Before the trumpeters on a ledge above the merchants and the group from Jebel ed Ben could take up the signal, the great crowd in the streets heard it. "Listen!" one cried, and a hush fell over them. Yes! They were less than five miles away!

The whole palace erupted with the sound of

brass instruments of all kinds and from every window. Blast after blast! Long blasts! Series of short blasts! Up and down blasts! Loud blasts! None soft! And the celebrants pressing and straining below attempted to do vocally what all the trumpets in Damascus were doing. Laughing, cheering, jumping, screaming! It was abandoned frenzy. Unleashed emotion! Uninhibited joy!

All at once the blowing stopped and this brought an unreal silence between the palace and the gates and every eye looked toward Israel. The gates were opening! Look! Look! It is the great one! It is Naaman! A chant began. "Naaman, the Great One! Naaman, the Great One!" One of the trumpets on the ledge above took up the tempo and accents of the chant and soon the whole city seemed to pound with the phrase, "Naaman, the Great One! Naaman, the Great One!"

At the city gates the horses with their important military men astride them kept the crowds away from their hero. Behind the horsemen was the large, glittering chariot of Benhadad. When Naaman and Jaichim and their escort of five riders came through the gates they dismounted at the sight of the king. Naaman and his group bowed before Benhadad and he walked over to Naaman and touched his shoulder. "Get up, Naaman! Get up and let me embrace you!" Naaman rose to his feet. Benhadad held him at arm's length and looked him over. The king could see Naaman was even more handsome than he was before he contracted leprosy. "Delivered! It is a wonderful word, my Captain," he said.

"Yes it is, my King!" answered Naaman, and they embraced.

A lesser officer came up and saluted Naaman and indicated he was to follow him to the king's chariot. Naaman stepped up in the chariot and the king handed a folded robe to the officer and he put it on Naaman; it was a robe of royal blue velvet richly decked with gold embroidery. Naaman looked around and spied Jaichim and motioned him to come to the chariot. Jaichim made his way to Naaman and Naaman reached down with his right arm and pulled Jaichim up into the chariot with him. "Come up with me, physician," he said, grinning.

Naaman's escort took their cue from the dismounted riders already inside the city and led their horses behind the chariot. Behind them a large canopied carriage was brought up and Benhadad and the queen were seated in that.

The noise of celebration prior to Naaman's appearance was but a murmur compared to the time of the parade. Ecstatic clamor poured forth in ever-increasing volume and Naaman received the plaudits with waves and smiles. Progress along the avenue was very slow and the king sometimes feared for the lives of some of the people. Farther on toward the palace he feared for the safety of Naaman, the hero. Finally, he began to fear for his own life and that of the queen. He was much relieved when they were all able to ascend the steps to the large platform that had been erected and covered with brightly colored fabric for the occasion. However, the queen was escorted into the palace and went up to join Mahrrah on the parapet.

The chamberlain had stayed by the steps to the platform during the parade waiting for the king to arrive. He was next to go up the steps after the king and Naaman. Jaichim followed the chamberlain and several dignitaries followed him. Seeing their hero and king together on the platform the crowd cheered loudly again but soon became quiet, expecting something to be said.

The chamberlain stepped forward and proclaimed in long, loud tones, "Citizens of Damascus, his most excellent ruler and potentate, Benhadad, King of Syria!" The great throng cheered as Benhadad stepped forward and the chamberlain retreated a few steps. The king finally held up his hands in a jesture that beckoned the people to be quiet and soon they were ready to listen again.

"Loyal and devoted subjects," the king began loudly and distinctly, "for this miraculous occasion on which we are welcoming home the most famous man in all Syria, Naaman, Captain of the King's Hosts . . . ." The king's last four words were lost in the thunder of the applause. He was a good five minutes restoring quiet. "For this occasion, I say, and in celebration of Naaman's recovery from his disease, I have commanded that several royal decrees be read for all to hear!" Again the applause was loud and continuous.

The king's chamberlain stepped forward with a large jeweled scroll and unrolled it to a length fitting the importance of the decrees and began reading.

"Benhadad, King of Syria, to all his subjects: Hear ye, hear ye my decrees. I hereby declare this day shall be called now and henceforth the Day of Naaman. This day shall be observed now and hereafter as a holiday throughout Syria. No one shall labor on the Day of Naaman, but it shall be a day of festivities for all. Upon this day ye shall take food and clothing to certain areas that shall be named where lepers will gather to receive the gifts."

The idea was charming. The reading was interrupted by applause that turned into chanting: "Day of Naaman! Day of Naaman!"

The chamberlain continued: "On this first Day of Naaman it is very fitting that some people who were responsible for uncovering a plot against your king's life be especially honored." Again, sustained applause.

"I decree that the merchants Wadi, Tawfik and Butros be hereafter known as 'The Royal Merchants' and that their store will henceforth be known as 'The Royal Bazaar'."

Benhadad turned his face to where he knew the merchants would be, above and to his left, and pointed toward them. The crowd cheered, "Royal Merchants!" and the three partners waved to the crowd below.

"It is duly noted that servants of the household of Naaman were equally responsible in foiling the attempt on the king's life: Abu, the chief steward, and Joseph, his assistant. It is now time to reward them. Abu and his wife, and Joseph, his assistant are no longer slaves but are declared free."

The crowd went wild, screaming and jumping up and down. Many of them knew Abu and started chanting, "Abu! Abu!" Again, Benhadad pointed to the parapet and Abu and Joseph waved and urged Gherza to join them. All on the great outer balcony were weeping and laughing.

Joseph called to Little One, "Little One, is it not wonderful?"

All she could do was answer joyfully, "Yes, Joseph, yes!"

When the great audience became quiet again, the chamberlain read on. "Should the servants I have named so choose, they may stay on in their present household at a worthy salary paid from the royal treasury." More wild applause.

After a bit the chamberlain was able to proceed. "The servant Joseph, previously mentioned, has a sister who is a servant in the same household. She is called Little One. Little One shared with us the good news there was deliverance for Naaman to be found in Samaria." The huge gathering exploded. "Little One! Little One!" they chanted. Joseph sat her on the apron of the parapet and held her tightly so she could wave to the crowd. By now they had learned the honored ones were all 40 feet or so above them, and all their eyes were focused on the tiny figure in the sky-blue robe waving back at them.

The chamberlain went on, "It is hereby decreed that Little One is no longer a slave, but is a free citizen." Again the speaker was forced to stop reading while the throng gave vent to ecstatic delight.

"Little One shall be asked to stay on as a paid employee and a valued member of the-household of Naaman and Mahrrah, friends of the king!"

There was more cheering and more speaking; speaking and cheering. Finally the celebrants began thinning out and going to their homes where they cooked good things to eat; plenty for themselves and plenty for the lepers, too. They rummaged through garments that were still good and sound but that they had grown tired of and set them aside to take along with the food. The bazaar would be doing a good business the next few days; many citizens got carried away with their spirit of generosity and gave more than they intended.

Naaman and Mahrrah embraced and ran bashfully to where she had spent the three nights waiting word from the caravan about Naaman and closed the door behind them.

Soon they were back out with their children, trusted servants and friends, including King Benhadad and his queen.

"Your highess," said Naaman, "my eternal gratitude for your constant care of my family and for sending me to Samaria for deliverance is beyond my ability to express. Thank you, your majesty! Thank you!" And Naaman and his wife bowed their heads in gracious respect before their king.

Benhadad replied with several appropriate words and asked them to stay for dinner, but Naaman said, "Sir, let me and my family go home today. I have never been inside the great house at Jebel ed Ben. Let my first night in Damascus since my cleansing be at home where I've longed for years to be."

King Benhadad understood and hastened off to give the orders needed for getting them back to Jebel ed Ben. Since coming into the palace, Naaman had eyes only for Mahrrah, but now he had time to greet his children and meet the others his wife had told him about when they met at the festival. Mahrrah pointed each one out to him.

"Abu and Gherza!" Naaman said, "Yes, and Joseph. How can I thank you for such devotion to my family? Yes, and to my king also! I rejoiced in the king's decree concerning you." The three ex-slaves bowed and murmured modest replies.

"Ah!" said Naaman when Little One was introduced to him. "So this is the little flower of Israel that brightened the sad halls of my home while I was away from my family and is most responsible for my recovery!"

Little One, somewhat embarrassed by all this, recovered enough to say, "Sir, I knew the God of Israel was able to heal you through His man Elisha. It is good to have you home."

Naaman was struck by her seriousness. "Yes indeed, Little One, and our home is truly your home now, and we shall have many hours for you to tell all of us everything you know about that wonderful man Elisha and about the great God he serves, for his God and your God is my God now."

Then came the voice of Benhadad from the hallway.

"And now," said Naaman, "the king is calling. Let us all go home."

☙

THE END

☙